A PERFECT BOWL OF PHO

A PERFECT BOWL OF PHO

NAM NGUYEN

PLAYWRIGHTS CANADA PRESS
TORONTO

For professional or amateur production rights, please contact the Playwrights Guild of Canada: St. Matthew's Clubhouse, 450 Broadview Ave., Toronto, ON M4K 2N1
416.703.0201 | orders@playwrightsguild.ca

If you're actually reading this, tag @wilfredmoeschter in a selfie with this book on Instagram and tell him he owes you $5 or a bubble tea. (note: not legally binding)

LIBRARY AND ARCHIVES CANADA CATALOGUING IN PUBLICATION
Title: A perfect bowl of pho / Nam Nguyen.
Names: Nguyen, Nam (Playwright), author.
Description: A play.
Identifiers: Canadiana (print) 20210305657 | Canadiana (ebook) 20210305673
  | ISBN 9780369102348 (softcover) | ISBN 9780369102355 (PDF)
  | ISBN 9780369102362 (HTML) | ISBN 9780369102379 (Kindle)
Classification: LCC PS8627.G86 P47 2021 | DDC C812/.6—dc23

Playwrights Canada Press operates on Mississaugas of the Credit, Wendat, Anishinaabe, Métis, and Haudenosaunee land. It always was and always will be Indigenous land.

We acknowledge the financial support of the Canada Council for the Arts, the Ontario Arts Council (OAC), Ontario Creates, and the Government of Canada for our publishing activities.

in memory of Nguyễn Bá Tứ (1937–2020)
a poet and a refugee
who wouldn't let me be first in the family to publish
and rudely beat me there by twenty-eight years

Good food is like music you can taste, colour
you can smell. There is excellence all around
you. You need only be aware to stop and
savour it.

—Auguste Gusteau, *Ratatouille*

I can still smell the fire
Though I know it's long died out
The smoke still hangs in my hair
And on some quiet evenings it burns my eyes

So darlin', play your violin
I know it's what you live for
Darlin', play your violin
We will manage somehow.

—Mitski Miyawaki,
"Because Dreaming Costs
Money, My Dear"

Look at this pho—

—Chad Kroeger

A PERFECT BOWL OF PHO

TABLE: *of contents*

Qty. Số Lượng	Description Món Ăn	Amount Giá Tiền

Thank you

	TOTAL	18.95

what a
steal!

A PERFECT PHO-WORD
BY DAVID YEE

In 2017 I was asked to adjudicate the University of Toronto's Drama Festival at Hart House Theatre. As with many of my celebrity appearances and endorsements, I was prepared to do the bare minimum required to collect my exorbitant fee and not a hair more.[1] However, this particular year, I was moved for the first time to award a production based on merit. From the first metatheatrical gag to the final emotionally manipulative song, *A Perfect Bowl of Pho* was able to accomplish something that had long been considered impossible: it made me pay attention.

"Sometimes there are plays that are so thrilling, theatrically, that watching them feels cathartic; a sacred experience from which you emerge a changed and better person." That's how my play was described by the adjudicator when it won the Best Production[2] award at the U of T Drama Festival in 1999.

Bestowing the same award upon Nam Nguyen and his band of musical misfits—while nowhere near the same degree of prodigiousness as my previous (and rather effortless) accomplishments—was still quite a feather in their caps.

The play I saw that night was not the same play you hold in your hands now. Even the version that I generously presented through my

---

1   In these situations, I generally award student productions alphabetically, the top prize going to the play with the title closest to the letter A, and so on. Alternately, if available, I could also throw the house programs down a flight of stairs and grant awards based on where they land.

2   It also won Outstanding Technical Achievement, Outstanding Performance, and the Most Handsome Playwright awards, essentially sweeping the categories that year.

company, fu-GEN Theatre, wasn't the same as either of the other iterations. Between the drama festival and the professional debut, I sat down
with Nguyen to ask him a few questions about the play, his plans for
it, what it could become. That conversation was then dramatized and
included *in* the play—a shameless effort to capitalize on my hard-earned
stardom,[3] and another opportunity for Nguyen's beloved metatheatri-
cality. Reductive as his rendition of the conversation is, he's right about
one thing: I pushed him for a meaning that was deeper (and more
truthful) than "I'm funny." And despite his performative protestations
within the metanarrative he created, I think he's pulling a bit of a fast
one. Or, perish the thought, he might be smarter than he tells us he is.[4]

Nguyen tells us this is a play about phở, that it is—unequivo-
cally—not about refugee trauma or immigrant grit, that it is most
certainly a play about consumption. Now, I'm not a theatre scholar
with half a PH.D., like Guillermo Verdecchia . . . I'm just a regular guy.
I'm like any of you: a devilishly handsome Olympic silver medallist
for rhythmic gymnastics turned Navy Seal turned multi-award-win-
ning playwright. But even I can tell you that Nguyen isn't entirely
right. While the play might literally be *about* consumption, it holds
all those other truths inside of it. Even if phở (the food) is somehow
divorced from its emblematic symbology, *Pho* (the play) becomes
the greater cultural signifier of Vietnamese-ness. Or, to be slightly
cliché about it: the sum is greater than its parts.

The reason the play has been through so many iterations isn't just
because Nguyen—as author—is fundamentally restless and perpetually
unsatisfied,[5] it's also because Nguyen—as cultural anthropologist—
is constantly evolving his own understanding of Vietnamese-ness,

---

3   Though, for legal reasons, I am only referred to as the "VIP" (whom he attests
is an amalgam of several different people, but we both know it's really just me).

4   While still not being as smart as he thinks he is.

5   I don't know Nguyen enough to categorically say this is true . . . luckily one
doesn't need a strong basis of familiarity in order to make wild accusations that
turn out to be eerily accurate.

Asian-ness, Other-ness. The development of this work hasn't been in pursuit of Importance;[6] rather, it's been in service of a cultural, emotional, and even spiritual truth. That truth may not be universal in a wholesale kind of way, but it is *Nguyen's* truth. And the delivery of it inside a razzle-dazzle musical package rife with double (or, in many cases, single) entendres, facile pop culture references, and dubious rhyming schemes alongside its scathing critical ethnography makes that truth all the more complicated and authentic, and even truthier.[7]

The autoethnography at work in *Pho* isn't the same earnest stuff behind the identity plays of the nineties, though they share the same hallmarks. Food being one of them. There's been a fair amount of critical research on the topic of food in those early artistic works, its importance in defining, maintaining, and celebrating difference in identity. Food is, for many diaspora outside the majority culture, emblematic of *home*. While in some cases, like phở, it has also become a part of the majority culture's emblematic identifiers of *away* or *other*. This contradiction and its attendant trappings is often a crisis point in the personal formation of an authentic cultural subjectivity. We see it in *Pho* as we see it in Leon Aureus's *Banana Boys* as we see it in Jovanni Sy's *A Taste of Empire* as we see it in Rick Shiomi's *The Walleye Kid* as we see it in *Gold Mountain Restaurant Montagne d'Or*, Karen Tam's exhibition at MAI. Food is not, as Nguyen feigns to suggest, simply transactional, its message inextensive beyond itself. Rather, the food of our people contains the blueprint to our culture. Its past and its future.

The post-migrant theatre Nguyen subscribes to eschews the earnestness of its forebearers in favour of something louder, messier, more complicated, less sentimental, rowdier, uncompromising, and wilful in its disobedience of classical storytelling. *Pho*'s narcissism and irrepressibility are part and parcel of its post-migrant identity, distractions that belie its

---

6 As one might suspect given his metatheatrical ponderances in the third act.

7 The fact that I don't get a squiggly red underline on the word "truthier" terrifies me, as it should my editor. Let's see if he notices.

hidden depths and cultural interrogation. The *character* of Nguyen's inability to find meaning is at the core of its actual *meaning*. Like its eponymous dish, the play is deceptively simple, and its narrator wildly unreliable.

Then again, what do I know? I'm just a handsome man trying to make it in the world as the real-life inspiration for a major character in Stephanie Meyers's classic *Twilight* series of novels.[8]

And the rest is up to you, fair reader. As you nose through these pages[9] I trust you'll draw your own conclusions, but I hope some of you will see what I did at that drama festival in 2017: that Nguyen, though an abject failure as a person, may just be the defining voice of his generation of artists.

To paraphrase Cary Grant in *Casablanca*: he's the hero they deserve.[10]

David Yee
Seychelles, 2021

David Yee is a mixed race (half Chinese, half Scottish) playwright and actor, born and raised in Toronto. He is the co-founding artistic director of fu-GEN Theatre Company, Canada's premiere professional Asian Canadian theatre company. A Dora Mavor Moore Award–nominated actor and playwright, his work has been produced internationally and at home. He is a two-time Governor General's Literary Award nominee for his plays lady in the red dress *and* carried away on the crest of a wave, *which won the award in 2015 along with the Carol Bolt Award in 2013. He has worked extensively in the Asian Canadian community as an artist and advocate.*

---

8   "Novels" is, admittedly, a strong word.

9   Undoubtedly in the clearance bin of a local Chapters / Indigo.

10   While commonly attributed to *Casablanca* in popular culture, this quote is actually from the 2008 film *The Dark Knight*. Also, it was Humphrey Bogart in *Casablanca*, not Cary Grant. That was a test and you failed.

PREFACE

There are many stories about Vietnam and food that didn't make it into the play, and here's one: Nguyễn Cơ Thạch grew up under French rule in Nam Định province, the birthplace of pho. He was fourteen years old when he joined the anti-colonial revolutionary war, and still only in his late twenties when the revolution succeeded. So in 1954, the new communist government of North Vietnam started appointing their party members to all the roles of governance, and Thạch made the sudden career pivot from guerilla soldier in a jungle to diplomat in an office, with all its foreign languages and etiquette standards that Thạch would have to pick up on the job. Thạch soon went on his first diplomatic visit to India—also the first time he ever left Vietnam—where he found himself in an interesting predicament. See, France invented fine dining, but sharing it with the poors and the ethnics of the empire like Thạch was low on their priority list. Now, this son of Vietnamese peasants was seated at his first formal dinner at New Delhi's French embassy, wearing a borrowed suit, and on the table in front of him Thạch found no chopsticks, but rather a fork and a knife, which he had no clue how to use.

Another story, a few decades later and an ocean away: I have a nephew, Joe, who we could say is Vietnamese like Thạch. Joe has his own set of perspectives and problems as a Canadian-born middle-schooler, though, and at least for now he's quite uninterested in "the homeland culture." One day, while we were quarantined together during the COVID-19 pandemic, Joe asked to borrow my wireless computer mouse so that he could better play *Team Fortress 2*. But I know that Joe likes to snack on chips while gaming, and I didn't want chip grease or Cheeto dust on my mouse. Thus, Joe found himself in his own predicament when I saw the family learning opportunity here. I told Joe that I'm happy to loan him my mouse anytime, provided he eats his chips using *these*—then I handed him a pair of chopsticks, which of course he had no clue how to use.

I like how these stories kinda rhyme, for all the physical, temporal, political, and cultural distance between them. A simple utensil turns the mundane act of eating into the pivotal moment of a small, self-contained drama. Better learn quick, lads!

I'm coming up on the age of twenty-four as I write this introduction, and I've been working on the musical it precedes in some capacity since the summer I turned nineteen. I recognize that it's because I'm young, but these five years have felt long, so it's personally momentous for me. My heartfelt thanks to the many actors, musicians, directors, music directors, designers, stage managers, and admin teams who've worked on each iteration of *Pho* up to now, at the Victoria College Drama Society, the Paprika Festival, fu-GEN Theatre Company, and the Toronto Fringe Festival. In the early stages of writing back in 2016, I also had a habit of asking everyone I knew if they had an interesting pho story from their personal lives, and I'm very grateful for anyone who told me anything, even though the vast majority of it didn't end up in here—with three notable exceptions in Scenes Five, Seven, and Twelve, and y'all know who you are. (Unfortunately, that one food poisoning story that involved attempting to unclog a toilet with your bare hands did not make the final cut, so apologies to that guy, for several reasons.) All of you have helped make the show into what it is today—though not as much as I helped make the show what it is today. I have the over one hundred .docx files to prove it, and this book is probably the final version of all of those.

The cuisine depicted, though, is firmly unfinalized. That's because Vietnamese people and Vietnameseness keep changing—from Thạch to Joe, from the ancient king Lang Liêu to my father, from the unnamed inventor of pho to the refugees who opened its first international restaurants. In all these peoples' lives, and yours as well, eating is not optional, but what we eat and how is something we decide from whatever ingredients that history hands us. Unfortunately, while time goes on and Viet cuisine can remain a work-in-progress forever, I had a measly five years to write and I need to submit this manuscript in about three months ago, so these twelve scenes will cover what they can, as they are. But they're, like, funny, and there's singing, so try to enjoy yourself?

For what it's worth, Thạch skipped the dinner's first course to simply observe how the other diplomats ate, and he ended up mastering Western cutlery by the entree. He told that story to a New York audience many years later, probably with some embellishments, after he'd ascended to the office of Foreign Minister of a unified Vietnam. Meanwhile, Joe still complains about chopsticks, but he's much better at using them than he admits. We always work it out.

—Nam

PRODUCTION NOTES

This is a musical comedy. A band plays music and singers sing the music. It moves fast.

This play can be performed with a minimum of seven actors and some very clever double casting. More actors will give you more flexibility. Actor-musicians are the stuff of dreams.

This play requires real bowls, real chopsticks, and a majority of real Asian actors—not metaphorical ones. Visit an old-school Vietnamese restaurant near you, spend a lot of money there, and take notes on how things look.

Real food, maybe even to share with the audience, would be swell if your venue allows it.

Accents and pronunciation choices mark generational differences between characters. Words rendered with diacritics (e.g., "phở") should be pronounced in a Vietnamese way, but without diacritics they become casual English readings (e.g., "pho" is generally pronounced "*foh*"), like Nam almost always says, even though he knows better.

Text **bolded** this way was originally projected or written on poster board. Keep what you like and display it however you can, and feel free to add any other historical notes you deem necessary for your audience.

A Perfect Bowl of Pho was first professionally produced on January 24, 2019, by Hotake Theatre and presented by fu-GEN Theatre Company at the Factory Studio Theatre, Toronto, in a double bill with *Fine China* by Julie Phan. It featured the following cast and creative team:

Music by Wilfred Moeschter and Nam Nguyen
Additional music by Sam Clark

Company: Meghan Aguirre, Max Gu, Kenley Ferris-Ku, Sai Lian Macikunas, Victoria Ngai, Nam Nguyen, Justin Park, Jacob Peng, Julie Phan, Lucinda Qu, Brendan Rush, Kenzie Tsang

Keyboard: Rena Seeger
Flute: Joey Zhuang
Violin 1: Randy Chang
Violin 2: Charlotte Wong-Labow
Cello: Brendan Rogers
Percussion: Keshav Sharma-Jaitly

Director: Gianni Sallese
Music Director: Kevin Vuong
Assistant Music Director: Kevin Yue
Producer: Kevin Yue
Stage Manager: Emma Monet
Production Manager: Deborah Lim
Costume Design: Bailey Hoy
Lighting and Projection Design: Abby Palmer
Property Master: Jasmine Cabanilla
Publicist: Wilfred Moeschter
Treasurer: Thomas Zheng

CAST

Amy	Kevin
An	Khang
Bach	Lang Liêu
Bắt Lơ	Leo
Bib	Miss Jones
Camera Operator	Nai
DJ	Nam
Dọn Dẹp	Nam's Dad
Driver	Nam's Mom
Duong	Nấu Gì
Farmer	Nhung
Generic Country Singer	Noah Lotaboutpho
Grenouille	Owner
Heo	Tên Nít
Influencer	Thang
Jen	Tuyet
Jen's Mom	VIP

SCENE ONE:
THE ANSWER

in which the show begins, and we discover the universal solution to Vietnamese problems

A poor FARMER *in northern Vietnam, donning loose-fitting clothes and a rice paddy hat, wallows over his misfortune. A flute or zither echoes his operatic wailing, utterly classical in technique.*

FARMER: *(sings)* I dreamed I was a king in sorrow
For a stranger stole my crown, my land, my grain
I dreamed a wave would come tomorrow
To drown me and relieve me of my pain[1]

Then I awoke, and sadly spoke
"My nightmare ends, but still I suffer now"
I am no king, but I lost everything—
When the white man ate my only cow[2]

---

1   The flute part here plays the melody to "Qua Cầu Gió Bay," a northern Vietnamese folk song.

2   This is usually the first laugh, though we got the odd chuckle from the mere sight of a rice paddy hat at the top. Obligatory fragment of "Dies irae" in the flute part, of course.

And with no cow, how shall I plow?
If I can't plow, how shall I grow rice now?
If rice won't grow, how can I feed a home
Of seven children with only cattle bones?

This last crop was nothing to admire
With these bones, they're my only supplies[3]
My feet on the fire, my need is quite dire
Is an answer in front of my eyes?

> NAM *and* KEVIN *appear at a table, waiting for food at a modern Toronto Viet restaurant. Like the* FARMER, NAM *is also Viet and poor, but as a contemporary Canadian student. His friend* KEVIN *is considerably more put together.*

KEVIN: Nam, where's the play?

NAM: Ugggh!

> *Music shift—suddenly big and show-tuney, but with the same flute melody beneath.*[4]

---

3   The flute part here is "Sunayama," a really lovely early-twentieth century song by Japanese composer Shinpei Nakayama, which I encountered in a setting called "Fantasy on a Japanese Folk Song" by American composer Samuel Hazo for high school band. This isn't some oblique reference to Japan–Vietnam relations, though, it just sounds nice.

4   I knew just enough about slapping words to melodies and chords to write the Farmer's lament myself, but most of the music from here is the work of my "co"-composer Wilfred Moeschter. We had a lot of input over the years from successive music directors and band members, though—for example, the basic sound of this latter portion of "The Answer" was set in 2017 by our guitarist Sam Poole (thanks to whom *Pho* will always have some ginger in it).

(sings) I dreamed I was a burnt-out student
Who once upon a time thought he was smart
I dreamed, or rather, self-deluded
That the best way I could spend my time is art

NAM: *(sings)* Then I awoke, and
sadly spoke
This is no dream, you lazy shit,
the world is waiting!

> KEVIN: That's a bit dramatic.

My roommate goes—

> I'm Kevin, by the way—
> *(sings)* Nam, you should write
> a show

But I instead just keep on
procrastinating

> Type something out

But what about

> Forget your doubt

This writer's drought?

> And do it quick

Go eat a dick! Be patient

> We're losing patience
> You've had all year

Don't rush me here!
And before I write, I need an
inspiration

> Just give me something here

Representation!

> Colonization!

Gentrification!

> Orientalization!

Something Asian?

Well, here's to hoping I'm
surprised

I'll surprise you![5]

FARMER, NAM, & KEVIN: *(sings)* My feet on the fire, my need is quite dire
Is an answer in front of my eyes?

Transgressing the barriers of time and space, the FARMER
passes by NAM *and* KEVIN'*s table with a steaming pot of promise.* NAM *fixates on this as* KEVIN *continues to berate him.*

FARMER: *(sings)* Broth from the
bones from the cow that they
felled

KEVIN: *(sings)* Write what
you know

Noodles of rice so it's something to sell

NAM & KEVIN: *(sings)* What do I/
you know?

The flavour's like nothing the
people would know

NAM: *(sings)* I know about . . .

But they'll cherish forever

KEVIN: *(sings)* The show's
about . . .

This soup I call . . . ![6]

---

5   IRL Kevin and I, singing our own roles here in 2017, had a good laugh
when we realized I'd copied the first four notes of "What You Own" from RENT
here—"don't breathe too deep!"

6   Coincidentally, you can kinda sing the Farmer's lyrics here to the tune of
"My Favorite Things."

NAM: *(sings)* Welcome to the show about . . . !

KEVIN: *(sings)* Welcome to the show about . . . !

The music stops.

NAM: So! Should I get the tripe? I don't know.

KEVIN: Huh?

NAM: Yeah, it's a tripe kinda day.

> *NAM jots his order down on an order sheet on the restaurant table. A waiter comes to take it away.*

KEVIN: Great. So, are we gonna talk about . . . ?

NAM: About?

KEVIN: Your play idea?

NAM: Ah, I shoulda got the tendon! What?

KEVIN: Your play idea!

NAM: Oh. Right. I don't have one.

KEVIN: You invited me to lunch just to tell me you came up with nothing?

NAM: No. I invited you to lunch 'cause I'm hungry.

KEVIN: I gave you all summer to think of ideas!

NAM: That's plenty of time.

KEVIN: Nam, it's the middle of September. Class starts on Monday.

NAM: Oh.

KEVIN: Yeah.

NAM: Oh, *shit*.

    Beat.

I forgot, I wanted an avocado milkshake.

KEVIN: Goddammit, Nam, I'm talking about something important—

NAM: So am I!

KEVIN: What?

NAM: Food. Specifically, Vietnamese food.

KEVIN: Vietnamese food is *not*—

NAM: Uh, pre-emptively take back the dumb thing you were about to say about my culture, you Chinese supremacist bitch.

KEVIN: *Hong Kong* supremacist, thank you. And I *like* Vietnamese food. But you know what I'd like more?

NAM: Dim sum?

KEVIN: I think I'd *like* it if you wrote a damn play for the U of T Drama Festival so that you don't stay indoors for another year being a self-pitying asshole.

NAM: Well, when you put it like that—go fuck yourself. Idea will happen when it happens.

KEVIN: I'm disappointed in you.

NAM: I'm used to it.

KEVIN: Great.

> *A mutually annoyed silence. A waiter places two bowls of soup on NAM and KEVIN's table.*

Food's here.

NAM: Thank god.

> *NAM moves to eat, but starts staring deeply into the bowl. Music cue. An idea?*

Wait . . .

KEVIN: Huh? What's up?

> *NAM, still entranced by the bowl, picks up his chopsticks and snatches something out of the broth. The music stops.*

NAM: Ha, it was a mosquito. This place's standards are really dropping—

The FARMER erupts back onto the stage from somewhere improbable. The music starts again; everyone unblinkingly breaks back into song.

FARMER: *(sings)* This soup I call . . .

NAM: *(sings)* Welcome to the show about . . . !

KEVIN: *(sings)* Welcome to the show about . . . !

FARMER: Phở.[7]

Musical button.[8]

---

7   This rhyme-scheme killer should be a correct, even slightly exaggerated, pronunciation of phở in Vietnamese, which is more like "fuh?" and not "foh." No more pronunciation tips in the footnotes, though!

8   "The Answer" ends with the violins playing "mi-so-la" (it's in a minor key), and four years after writing it, Wilf and I retroactively decided that this was a subconscious reference to the original English-language *Pokémon* theme song. We can seed this play with however many antique folk melodies, but we're geeky '90s kids, and we'll always end up right back at the *real* song of our people.

SCENE TWO:
VIETNAM PIMPIN',
OR,
WORLD CULTURES DAY

notions of authenticity, ethnic pride, and resourcefulness in
between hot rhymes about pho, chả giò, and bánh chưng

The beginning of a dope beat plays in the background. MISS
JONES *enters a classroom with several students, including* JEN.

MISS JONES: Alright, class, remember that tomorrow is World
Cultures Day,[9] so I hope you're all ready to set up your country's
booths with your yummy, yummy foods!

The students cheer. JEN *emerges from them, screeching.*

JEN: YAAAAAAAAAAAAAAAH!

MISS JONES: Jen? Jen, I—Jen! I appreciate your enthusiasm, but—

JEN: Brap brap brap brap!

---

9   We once had Miss Jones unroll a World Cultures Day poster here featuring
one of Prime Minister Justin Trudeau's more "colourful" outfits during his trip
to India. Shame that the 2019 brownface scandal hadn't popped up yet.

The dope beat goes ham. JEN *terrorizes her classmates,*
destroying the room in the process.

(raps!) Yo, there's a shark in the water, oughtta get outta the pool
Viet daughter 'boutta bring the hottest stand to the school
I tell ya, other bitches better be prepared for a beatin'
Because it ain't World Cultures Day until somebody is bleedin'

Best prepare for meat-eating, it don't bear no repeating
I'm speeding down the list of reasons why my feast be leading

JEN: *(raps)* I got some chicken	ENSEMBLE: What
Pork	What
And you know that we beefing	
And 'em spring rolls ready	
with a bit of reheating	

JEN: *(raps)* Pickle veggies on the side, milky coffee on the ice
Your pick of rice, fried or white, at no additional price
Not only that, I got a burner stove and cans of gas
So you can slurp a bowl of pho when I'm through kicking yo ass

Ho! So, you might as well not show
Hah, leave your dumb-ass perogies at home
Dunno how you always burn nachos
So just quit it, you'll be finished by these dishes I make all on my own

(speaks) With my mom's help.
She does the cooking.
I roll the spring rolls.
Bitch.

(raps) Vietnam pimpin', yo, stop yo bitchin'
I'm dishing out the dishes, fresh out the kitchen
Now I'm ready steady go, to go international
And I'm never going slow, I'm Vietnam pimpin'—

Jump to after school. JEN'S MOM *is driving* JEN *home.*[10]

JEN'S MOM: So tell me how you got detention.

JEN: Miss Jones says I "destroyed" "the classroom" "with enthusi-asm." And "made gratuitous use of the B-word."

JEN'S MOM: Jenny, again?

JEN: But it's okay! She let me keep my World Cultures Day booth! And tomorrow, we'll see who's giving who detention.

JEN'S MOM: That's not how that works.

JEN: Did you start the chả giò?

In case you didn't know: chả giò
a deep-fried spring roll, usually containing pork

JEN'S MOM: Yes, I finished them this morning.

JEN: Finished? But I wanted them fresh tomorrow . . .

JEN'S MOM: Huh?

---

10   Gianni Sallese's direction had all the vehicles in this show represented by actors holding Wii Wheels. We're just a bit ahead of the curve in tapping into that late-2000s nostalgia market.

JEN: Whatever. It's fine. What about the pickled carrots and radish?[11]

JEN'S MOM: You want those too? Honey, that's gonna take a whole day, at least.

JEN: Why didn't you start earlier, Mom?!

JEN'S MOM: I have work, Jenny!

JEN: At least tell me I'll have the pho!

**In case you didn't know: phở
a soup consisting of broth, rice noodles, herbs, and either beef
or chicken**

JEN'S MOM: Of course! I just came from the supermarket.

*JEN'S MOM gestures to a bag by the driver's seat. JEN pulls a
bag of broth powder out.*

JEN: Instant . . . broth . . . powder?! But I told everyone I was going to have authentic, slave-away-over-a-stove-for-eight-hours broth!

JEN'S MOM: It tastes the same.

JEN: No it doesn't! You ruin everything, Mom!

---

11   In case you didn't know, pickling is one of those things that started in India thousands of years ago and then spread across Asia via trade networks, kinda like Buddhism. I couldn't tell you for sure which of those things from India had the head start, but I suspect no one was volunteering for the vegetarian Buddhist life before pickles.

JEN throws a tantrum.[12] *JEN'S MOM tries to calm her down.*

JEN'S MOM: Jen! Jenny! JENNIFER![13]

JEN quiets down.

Aren't you taking World Cultures Day a little too seriously? What are you even getting from this?

JEN: The satisfaction of crushing my enemies. And a twenty-dollar gift card to McDonald's.

JEN'S MOM: Jenny. I'll take you to McDonald's myself if that's what you really want.

JEN: . . . That's not it. The other kids make fun of me at lunch-time. They see me with leftover noodles, and they all have . . . Lunchables.

In case you didn't know: Lunchables
how your parents tell you that they don't love you

JEN'S MOM: *(grimacing)* Lunchables.

JEN: I just wanted to show everyone our food is the best.

JEN'S MOM brings the car to a screeching halt.

---

12   Possibly:

JEN: I hate you I hate you I hate you! Ugh! World Cultures Day is ruined! Culture is dead and you killed it! I'm gonna get a rusty knife, sneak into your room in the middle of the night, and stabbity stabstabstab—

13   In this role, Victoria Ngai preferred to substitute "Jennifer!" with "Jenjamin!"

Why'd you stop the car, Mom?

JEN'S MOM: Because this is a *family learning opportunity*, Jenny.

JEN: But we're in the middle of the road—

Another DRIVER pulls up behind JEN'S MOM's car.

JEN'S MOM: Jenny—

DRIVER: BEEP!

JEN'S MOM: Our food is . . .

DRIVER: BEEEEEEEP!

JEN'S MOM: OUR FOOD IS HUMBLE! What do you have to—

DRIVER: GET OFF THE ROAD!

JEN'S MOM: GO AROUND! I'M TRYING TO TEACH MY DAUGHTER A FUCKING LIFE LESSON—

DRIVER: FUCK YOU!

JEN'S MOM: FUCK YOU! ĐỤ MÁ MÀY!

They continue screaming swear-laden ad libs at each other as the other DRIVER pulls around and exits.

Ahem. As I was fucking saying—what do you have to prove to all the white kids?

JEN: I didn't say they were white.

JEN'S MOM: But they are.

JEN: Okay, they are.

JEN'S MOM: When I was younger than you are now and our family came to Canada, kids then didn't like what I brought for lunch either. But your grandpa told me this story, and I think you should hear it too. Okay?

> JEN *nods. Music. A mimed re-enactment of the story of* LANG LIÊU *begins.*[14]

Once upon a time, there was a king of Vietnam who was growing quite old. He needed a successor but didn't know which of his twenty-one sons to pick. Vietnamese men: they get around.

JEN: Wha—?

JEN'S MOM: I don't know who your father is. Anyway: one of the youngest princes was named Lang Liêu, but he didn't live a life of luxury like his brothers. His mother died when he was young, and he led a simple life as a farmer. When the king decreed that the prince to succeed him would be he who presented the best

---

14   The planned *Pho* production for 2020 was sadly cancelled along with the rest of the Toronto Fringe Festival due to that COVID thing, but that summer we ended up creating a video presentation of excerpts from *Pho* for the online Fringe Collective instead. That included this section, read by Jasmine Cabanilla but with the usual mimed re-enactment replaced with seven beautiful illustrations by Khoa Dang, who I first met through U of T's Vietnamese Students' Association. With much of the world on pause, I was still thankful for the unexpected opportunity to collaborate with talented artists in the Vietnamese Canadian community that maybe I couldn't have otherwise.

food to honour their ancestors on Tết, all of Lang Liêu's brothers searched far and wide for exotic ingredients to make extravagant new dishes. Now, Lang Liêu couldn't afford to venture to foreign markets, but he was far craftier with what he had. These were ingredients that even the poorest in the kingdom could access— rice, pork, mung beans. Using only these, Lang Liêu created a rice cake called bánh chưng that he presented to the king.[15] The other princes laughed, but the king saw its meaning immediately—by using humble ingredients, Lang Liêu showed that he understood the conditions of his people, and paid respect to the land and ancestors from which we all came. And thus, Lang Liêu became the heir to the throne of Vietnam, and all Vietnamese people eat bánh chưng every Tết to this day. Now—do you know the moral of the story?

JEN: I think so. Don't worry about the pho broth, Mom. What I need—is to flex on these hoes with some banh chung!

JEN'S MOM sighs. Dope beat drops once again as JEN returns to her class the next day, again terrorizing MISS JONES.

(raps) Hold your nachos and perogies, I ain't give a shit, damn
What we got is no baloney, straight outta Vietnam
This southeast mouth won't tell you everything
So get it from my friend Lang Liêu, he's a king

LANG LIÊU makes a big damn entrance.

---

15   The original legend has Lang Liêu making two different rice cakes, actually: bánh chưng to represent the earth, and bánh giầy to represent the heavens. Also, he got the idea from a fairy who visited him in a dream—I cut a lot for conciseness. (A silly story for trilinguals: once in my childhood, my older sister was having trouble figuring out how to best render "bánh giầy" in a French writing assignment, and I helpfully offered the translation "pain de souliers.")

LANG LIÊU: *(raps)* Bow down in the presence of immortal king Lang Liêu
Prince among the peasants with a morsel for ya, brand new
I'm low in funds, but lemme show you what I can do
Make a little cake o' rice so tasty, I'mma grant you

Favour with your heritage, flavour on your tongue
When you labour over sticky rice and pork and bean of mung
These ingredients convenient to every single one
Of our people, dip it in fish sauce—

JEN: *(raps)* Nước mắm, bitch!

Vietnamese riches in the sauce of the fishes[16]
While yo shit is fuckin' ridiculous, you already know
We drop our enemy like we drop the pho,[17] hah?
You get it? One more time, I'll say it slow

*JEN'S MOM and LANG LIÊU's ancient posse enter, dancing like
an old-school rap music video.*

---

16 Nước mắm is worth a whole play on its own! Fish sauce and its more popular soy cousin are likely the descendants of an ancient Chinese fermented-soy/
fish combo sauce, probably invented to stretch limited supplies of salt, accord-
ing to Mark Kurlansky's *Salt: A World History*. While the Chinese dropped the
fish and kept the soy, we contrarian Viets did the opposite, starting a long and
proud tradition of dumping our rotting fish water on everything. Nước mắm
eventually spread back up to Guangdong and around Southeast Asia via Chinese
trade (yielding Thai nam pla and Filipino patis), and then to British colonizers
as kecap. A few hundred years of Anglo ingredient substitutions later and now
purged of its anchovy ancestry, kecap's legacy survives in the Western fridge
in the form of modern American tomato ketchup. That said, I will personally
report you for a hate crime if you put ketchup on bánh chưng.

17 Though he is ethnic Viet, Lang Liêu isn't a stickler about the pronunciation
of pho, as he precedes the inventions of both pho and the modern Vietnamese
language by approximately five thousand years. Also, most Vietnamese kings
could not rap, with the notable exception of MC Lê Lợi "The Liberator."

Vietnam pimpin', yo, stop yo bitchin'
We're dishing out the dishes and you're ripe for the pickin'
We are ready steady go, to go international
And we're never going slow, one more time, yo, we're—

JEN & LANG LIÊU: *(raps)* Vietnam pimpin', yo, stop yo bitchin'
We're dishing out the dishes, fresh out the kitchen
Straight flexin' on these hoes in *A Perfect Bowl Of Pho*
So welcome to the show, we're Vietnam pimpin'!

Musical button.

SCENE THREE:
LEO'S BIG BREAK,
OR,
THE FOOLS WHO DREAM

**in which soup is physically re-enacted and pronunciation is
irrelevant**

NAM and the entire Asian ensemble enters.

NAM: And now, a poem: pho!

> *A highly uncomfortable movement piece begins. They re-en-
> act soup. Lots of slurping sounds. Freaky improvised atonal
> music.*[18] *Everyone is way too into it.*

ENSEMBLE: The Vietnamese rice noodle soup!
Such secrets you conceal!
What wisdom in the spices
In each sip shall be revealed?

---

18   The actor's idea of a closing night prank is saying a wrong word or two on
stage. The music director's idea of a closing night prank is conspiring with the
whole band to play the Mii Channel Theme here. Fuck you, Shreya.

First tasted in the East
Now you tantalize the world!
We plunge into your salty depths
And find your hidden pearls

> *There is an unpleasant, ancient groan from the ensemble and band with every utterance of the word "pho" that follows.*

Awaken your senses!
From mysterious origins: a perfect bowl of pho!

> *The ensemble begins creating a bowl of pho with their bodies.*

PEAK THEATRE!!

The ceramic bowl that contains the pho!
The delicately balanced broth of the pho!
Flat rice noodles in the broth of the pho!
Thin slices of rare beef, the heart of the pho!

NAM: The sound of my ancestors groaning at how I pronounce pho!

> *A particularly angry groan.*

ENSEMBLE: Green onions! Basil! Bean sprouts! All in the pho!

> *LEO, the first white man we see in the show, emerges from the "bowl." His mere presence seems to colonize the stage.*

LEO: A giant cloud of pale white steam, rising from the pho!

The ensemble shrieks in horror, ending the poem.

NAM: How the fuck did you get in here?

LEO: *(in a bad Southern accent)* Now, Nam, don't act like you don't 'member me.

NAM: Wait. Oh no.

The ensemble whimsically exits.[19]

ENSEMBLE: Flashback flashback flashback flashback flashback...

NAM sits at an audition table.

NAM: One p.m., November 19th, 2016. With writer's block vanquished, I'm holding auditions for the first-ever production of *A Perfect Bowl of Pho* at the University of Toronto. Please clap.

KEVIN enters.

Kevin! You're right on time.

KEVIN: For what?

NAM: Auditions.

KEVIN: Auditions?

NAM: For my show about pho?

---

19   Ensemble Naruto run? Why not?

KEVIN: Your show about pho—a pho show?

NAM: Fo' sho', yo.

KEVIN: Oh no. So the *noodle musical*? It's real?

NAM: Yes! Follow me along the noodle of space and time as I explore the history, culture, and my personal experience of Vietnamese food. What did you think was happening here?

KEVIN: K-pop dance class?

NAM: Similar demographic. Wanna audition?

KEVIN: Nam, I'm not an actor.

NAM: But I wrote this role I think you'd be perfect for, Kevin.

KEVIN: Who is it?

NAM: Take a wild guess, *Kevin*.

KEVIN: . . . Am I the director?

NAM: Close enough.

> *KEVIN jumps behind the audition table.*

KEVIN: I'm the director now. Seamless transition.

NAM: Well, Mr. Director, now we just need our cast.

> *LEO enters, with panache.*

LEO: Hello!

KEVIN: Hi!

NAM: Uh, can I help you?

LEO: I sure hope so! My name's Leo—[20]

NAM: The washroom's right across the hall from where you came in.

LEO: Oh, thanks, but I went before.

NAM: Oh. Were you looking for Ned's Café?

LEO: No. This is the Goldring Music Room, right?

NAM: Yes, but you can't use it; we're holding an audition here—

 LEO whips out his headshot and resumé. KEVIN takes it.

LEO: Right! I'm here for that.

NAM: You're here? For auditions for *A Perfect Bowl of Pho*?

LEO: Yeah!

KEVIN: Great. And who are you going to be reading for?

LEO: I'm going to be reading for the role of "Name."

---

20 Leo was retroactively named after the first actor to play this role. When IRL Leo played him, he was named Connor, and before *that*, he was named Leonardo, so that came full circle nicely.

NAM: Ahhh. Sorry, I think we both misunderstood something here. This is a show about *Vietnamese* food.

LEO: Mhm?

NAM: You know, Vietnamese food. Food from Vietnam. The Southeast *Asian* country.

LEO: Yes.

NAM: Where *Asian* people live.

LEO: Yup.

NAM: *Asians*. You understand me?

LEO: Loud and clear.

NAM: Like, *ching chong ling long ting tong*—

LEO: I'm pretty sure that's racist!

NAM: It is! So you understand that we need a certain type of actor for this show.

LEO: That's what I heard. And yes, I *am* a student of Victoria College.

NAM: No, I meant—

KEVIN: We do have a Vic student quota.

NAM: Okay, but he's—we need to get rid of that joke before we leave U of T—look. We're looking for East and Southeast Asian actors. And you're white.

LEO: Oh! Oh . . .

KEVIN: His resumé's pretty impressive.

NAM: Kevin!

KEVIN: That's *Mr. Director*.

NAM: Mr. Director, white people star in every other show—

LEO: Not *Hamilton*—

KEVIN: That means he has star potential!

NAM: Oh god.

KEVIN: Let's give him a chance! Diversify the cast.

NAM: No!

LEO: This is just like *Hamilton* all over again!

NAM: Seriously, do you expect me to whitewash *myself*?

> *Music cue. Someone throws one of* NAM's *costume items on* LEO.

LEO (AS NAM): *(sings)* I dreamed I was a burnt-out student—

KEVIN: You're right, that's not doing it for me.

Music stops.

I see him as more of a farmer . . .

*Music cue. An ensemble member brings out the FARMER's
rice paddy hat and is about to put it on LEO. Then the music
stops as NAM quickly reacts.*

NAM: Hey—HEY! Don't start with that shit on campus in Toronto.
You think this is Queen's or something? Jesus.[21]

*The bearer of the rice paddy hat retreats into the wings, to
LEO's disappointment.*

KEVIN: Sorry, Leo, I guess that's it.

LEO: Aw!

NAM: Actually, there's one role he could fill . . .

LEO: There is?!

KEVIN: Great, then let's go with that!

NAM: I'm glad you think so, Kevin. Leo, I'd love to have you in the
show. To play Kevin.

LEO: Okay!

---

21 Say what you will about race in Toronto, but I've at least never heard of a
racism-themed costume party happening here. They probably wouldn't have
invited me, though.

KEVIN: Wait.

LEO takes on one of KEVIN's costume pieces.

I'm suddenly not okay with this!

NAM: Wow, Kevin, you're looking very conventionally handsome today.

LEO: I get that a lot.

NAM: Do something new with your race?

KEVIN: You're from Hong Kong!

NAM: You're from Missouri.

LEO: *(with bad Southern accent)* Darn tootin'. I'm from Missouri! And I gots some things to say about that.[22]

KEVIN: Do they even have pho in Missouri?!

NAM: Shh, stranger. Let Kevin speak.

LEO: I reckon . . .

(to audience, under spotlight) Representation's a real hot-button issue to everybody. In my own life, I feel it very personally, y'hear? In our arts and entertainment industry, always there's some sad imitation of me, struttin' about with a bad accent, behaving as

---

22   Missouri is not actually in the American South, so if it really bothers you, write in Alabama instead.

someone else thinks I would have in a very narrow portion of our history that they think "defines" me. But I dream—of more. When might I stop playing who you want me to be, and just be who I am—a Caucasian man? From Missouri?

NAM: Passionate. Inspiring. I'm inspired. You know, white Kevin—

LEO: Kevin Simpson Josephiah Beauregard Sessions the Third!

NAM: You deserve better than this. I'll write you a better role. A role you were born to play. I promise to write you a role that shows white people as you *truly* are.

(to audience) And I promise *that* line will pay off in seven scenes.

LEO: Boy, am I excited for that! Look, Ma, my big break!

   Music.

(sings) Here's to the fools who dream!
Crazy as they may seem![23]

KEVIN: Nam, I think this bit is over now.

NAM: That's for the best.

---

23   This is an interpolation from *La La Land*, but that's already a dated reference, so feel free to slot in the lyrics to whatever the hottest inspirational musical number is among the whites in your moment, as long as you can make it conform to 3/4 time to transition into the next song.

SCENE FOUR: SCRAPS

**in which Nam fails to kill his darlings, and the French colonial
legacy survives**

*NAM and KEVIN are at a piano, surrounded by many sheets
of paper. NAM starts to sing a jazzy number, which begins in
rubato, while KEVIN accompanies.*

NAM: *(sings)* I grappled a long time with drafting this song
I'm unsure that it's apt even now
To acc'rutely capture with interspersed laughter
A hist'ry more rich than "dead cow"

**In case you didn't know: French Indochina
the union of France's colonial territories in Southeast Asia,
including Vietnam, from 1887 to 1954**

Yes, the French occupied us from pasture to city
And though the times after were also unpretty
I bet what you know of this era's less sure
Than the well-covered subsequent war—*grrrrat!*

Though I penned many sketches, none were represent'ive
In the end to embody this age
But just to pass by it would be to deny
Its impact on the foods I've engaged

So in the interest of depicting the imperial mission—
Since every bit that I writ by itself's insufficient!—
The decision I mapped was the best, no doubt:
Make soup from the scraps that I couldn't throw out

> NAM *takes a few pages of script in his hand. The music shifts
> to a stricter, more upbeat tempo.*

Okay! Picture this: we're in the kitchen of a colonial villa in Hanoi.
Enter the master of the house and his native cook.

> *The bombastic Frenchman* GRENOUILLE *and the meek cook*
> NÂU GÌ *enter to enact the scene described.*[24]

GRENOUILLE: Garçon! Where are you?!

NÂU GÌ: Here, monsieur!

GRENOUILLE: Is it true, what the other servants told me?

NÂU GÌ: No, of course not! What *did* they tell you, monsieur?

GRENOUILLE: They told me for dinner last night, you committed the
gravest betrayal against our social order! You baked my bread—a
Frenchman's bread!—with rice flour! An inferior Oriental ingredient purchased from the peasants' market!

NÂU GÌ: Monsieur, I would never!

GRENOUILLE: Promise me.

---

24   Obviously, Grenouille is French for "large noodle."

NẤU GÌ: I promise!

GRENOUILLE: Look me in the eye and swear on your god, Confucius!

NẤU GÌ: He's more a philosopher, and Chinese—

GRENOUILLE: Swear it!

NẤU GÌ: I swear that I-I—oh, monsieur, you must understand, wheat is so scarce—

GRENOUILLE: You admit it?!

NẤU GÌ: I'm filled with guilt!

GRENOUILLE: Say it! Say it out loud!

NẤU GÌ: Fine! I baked your bread with rice flour. I've done it for years!

GRENOUILLE: How could you?! You know how we pride ourselves on pure white bread made from the finest wheat grown in Eurrrropa!

NẤU GÌ: I deserve the death penalty!

GRENOUILLE: You do! But as I represent the redeeming light of the empire, I'll give you a chance to make this up to me.

NẤU GÌ: Really, monsieur?

GRENOUILLE: Really! Next week, I make my big expedition to Angkor Wat in the jungles of Cambodia. Angkor *what* do you suppose I'll eat there?

NÁU GÌ: Whatever the Cambodians eat?

GRENOUILLE: No. I'm going to lug around a big sack of bread for days and eat mouldy fistfuls of it like a civilized person.[25] And you will bake every loaf for me with one hundred percent wheat flour, at your own expense!

NÁU GÌ: But, monsieur, the war in Europe has stopped imports, and wheat doesn't grow on this land—

GRENOUILLE: If I cared what the land thought, I wouldn't have colonized it.

NÁU GÌ: Okay, fair enough.

GRENOUILLE and NÁU GÌ *exit.*

NAM: So? Kinda fun, kinda informative.

KEVIN: We learn what the master eats but not the cook?

NAM: Yeah?

KEVIN: So . . . you're privileging the tastes of the colonizer?

NAM thinks, then crumples up the pages in his hands.

NAM: Aw.

NAM chucks the paper away and returns to the song.

---

25 Based on a true story mentioned in Erica J. Peters's *Appetites and Aspirations in Vietnam: Food and Drink in the Long Nineteenth Century.*

(sings) So I hate to ask, but if we hate to waste
Could I dust off my drafts, use the scraps on my plate
When maybe I ought to throw it all out—

KEVIN: *(sings)* And leave colonial process in doubt?

No!

NAM: *(sings)* As we keep on extracting the wheat from the chaff
And we plead that the past leads to reasons to laugh
Will we have something deep to convey
In the scraps of the Viet food musical play?

NAM picks out another set of pages.

KEVIN: Something new?

NAM: Okay, I got it now—enter this elderly woman, a real relic of pre-colonial Vietnam, who walks up to an enterprising young barista on the city sidewalk—

HEO and NAI enter.[26] Carrying a tray, NAI is selling phin-filtered coffee.

NAI: Cà phê sữa! Cà phê sữa! Super strong coffee that will fuel you through this fast-moving modern world!

HEO: Hey, bean juice guy! Remember me?

---

26 These names, meaning pig and deer, came from the online Fringe Collective production, where the old lady and the barista were portrayed respectively by a plush of Peppa Pig and a souvenir statuette of a moose in a Quebec sweater that I got on a school trip in grade seven. I did the silly voice performance for both characters.

NAI: Old lady—I told you that's not what it's called.

HEO: Whatever! It did a number on my bowels. I almost shit myself walking home last night! What was in that "cà phê"?

NAI: Just coffee and condensed milk.

HEO: Condensed milk?

NAI: Yes, from a condensed cow.

HEO: Milk is for babies! Why would you want to drink that?

NAI: It tastes great! The French do it all the time.

HEO: If the French told you to jump off a bridge, would you jump, huh?

NAI: That's ridiculous—

HEO: And what would this city look like if we all drank your "cà phê" and shit ourselves, everyone! Shit running *everywhere*!

NAI: The French don't shit themselves when *they* drink milk.

HEO: What?! How?

NAI: They say it's evolution. The French can drink milk because, thousands of years ago, a Frenchman thought, "Hey, I'm gonna suck on that cow's nipple."

HEO: That's disgusting.

NAI: That's their culture.

HEO: Oh, "their culture"! You know two thousand years ago, the Trưng sisters assembled an army of Vietnamese women and freed our land from the Chinese? That's *our* culture! But now—these new foreigners rule us and contaminate your mind in the public schools so you too love to suck cow nipples.

NAI: You're stuck in the past, bà già. The French have done us a lot of good. You're worried they'll tell us to jump off a bridge—they built all the bridges in Hanoi! And the sewers. And the opera house.

HEO: Oh—have *you* ever seen an opera?

NAI: No . . .

HEO: Then they've built us a whole lot of nothing! The sewers don't even run under our section of the city. Remember that, when you poison us all with your "cà phê" and everyone in the Old Quarter *shits all over the street*—it'll have nowhere to go!

HEO and NAI exit.

NAM: Eh? That one's got *discourse*. And this time it's all about Vietnamese tastes.

KEVIN: I wish *one* Vietnamese person had the taste to not put poop content in a show about food.

NAM: Food goes in one end, shit comes out the other—it's biology! And, and!—I am *not* compromising on representation for lactose intolerants!

KEVIN: *That's* the hill you're dying on?

NAM: *(frenetic)* Why'd the white man take over, Kevin? Why'd he get us hooked on cà phê sữa đá just so I gotta pay him *fifty cents* for lactase pills every time I have dairy?! It's a fucking *conspiracy*, Kevin! WAKE UP!

    NAM and KEVIN return to the song.

(sings) So I hate to ask, but if pages were pulled
Straight out of my ass, would the masses indulge

KEVIN: *(sings)* When maybe the answer's to throw it away

NAM: *(sings)* But what would my ancestors say?

KEVIN: *(sings)* 'Cause would it be half as gripping if the drink is still dripping

NAM: *(sings)* And I mention up front that this thing's never done

NAM & KEVIN: *(sing)* Can we come up with something to say

KEVIN: *(sings)* In the scraps of the Viet food musical—

    NAM picks out another bit of script, waving it proudly.

NAM: This is it! This is the one!

    KEVIN takes the pages and skims them.

KEVIN: What? No, this is just . . . stupidly convoluted.

NAM: No no, there's something in this story, I can feel it.

KEVIN: How would you even go about explaining this to someone in point form?

NAM: Well, I think . . .

> *DỌN DẸP, BẮT LỞ, and TÊN NÍT gather around a fancy dinner table. They all present as members of French high society at first. They don't enact the scene so much as they go through the motions of it while describing it in short.*

CHORUS: *(sings)* Paris in my sight is shining
As bright as day from far away and never tiring
Oh, my heart will never stray
From those bistros and cafés

Paris, there is no comparin'
Simply the best so all the rest appear as barren
And if it were up to me
French is what I'd want to be[27]

DỌN DẸP: Oh hon hon! We are a high-class French family having a steak dinner party!

NAM: I'm condensing here—plot twist!

BẮT LỞ: Oh, what are we doing? We're really just rich Vietnamese Francophiles making fools of ourselves!

---

27   The melody here is lifted from a popular French song of the imperial age called "La Petite Tonkinoise," known as "Pretty Little Tonkin Girl" in English. It's a "love song" about a Vietnamese girl and it's aged hilariously poorly—the English lyrics are the first place I ever encountered the racial slur "Chinee."

NAM: But then another twist:

TÊN NÍT:[28] We're not even rich; we're poor house servants who are role-playing as rich in our French master's dining room while he's on an overnight trip![29] We don't even know how to eat steak!

NAM: Then, naturally:

> GRENOUILLE *enters and acts surprised to see the servants there.*

GRENOUILLE: What?! I leave for one night to visit the Michelin Rubber Plantation I operate here in Indochina, and I return home to find my servants treating the place like a Michelin restaurant!

NAM: 'Cause Michelin the tire company and Michelin that gives out stars to fancy restaurants are the same—

KEVIN: Yeah, I know—

NAM: And this is a metaphor—imperial labour is the basis of French fine dining—

KEVIN: I get it![30]

---

28   "Dọn dẹp" is Vietnamese for "clean up." "Bắt lơ" is a bad Vietnamese corruption of "butler," and "tên nít" is the same for "tennis." They were a maid, a butler, and a ball girl in the original version of the scene.

29   *Parasite* is a very good film, which I mention for no particular reason. That said, Vietnamese servants getting drunk in their absent French masters' villas was apparently a common enough occurrence for French dudes of the era to write it down, which also earns a mention in Erica Peters's book.

30   Sometimes people don't connect that Michelin tires and Michelin stars are from the same company, which I wouldn't blame you for. Makes sense, though, when

NAM: And then the real plot twist:

> BIB—*the Michelin Man, in full costume!—pops up out of nowhere, with a machete! Everyone screams!*

BIB: I'm the Michelin Man, but my real backstory is I was an indentured labourer on that rubber plantation before I got caught in a horrific latex refining accident and now I'm out for blooood.[31]

> BIB *gives the other in-scene characters a good horror movie chase.*

KEVIN: I think you're gonna lose people there.

NAM: Don't worry—right after the slasher flick part this is all revealed to be a very elaborate ad for a modern French Vietnamese restaurant that flaunts colonial imagery as a marketing gimmick.[32] It's deep!

---

you think about star ratings as a way to encourage the middle class to buy tires and go out on long car trips to top-tier restaurants. On the flip side of this, around the time Michelin invented their star system, they were overseeing some truly appalling abuses of tens of thousands of starving rubber plantation labourers in colonial Vietnam to supply their French tire factories. It's no surprise that those plantations were hotbeds of communist recruitment and revolt from the 1920s straight through to 1975. Also unsurprising: Michelin does not like to talk about this.

31   The official name of that big anthropomorphic stack of white tires we call the Michelin Man is Bibendum. His name comes from the Latin toast "nunc est bibendum," meaning "now is the time to drink," which appeared alongside Bib's first ad to mean that Michelin tires would "drink up" all the obstacles on the road. Neat coincidence, though, that the Latin quote comes from Horace's *Odes*, specifically the poem calling on Rome to drink to celebrate Octavian's recent victory over Cleopatra, the East finally conquered by the Empire . . .

32   See also Soleil Ho's restaurant review in the *San Francisco Chronicle*, "Le Colonial Is an Orientalist Specter," though flaunting colonial history is something that happens within modern Vietnam just as much.

KEVIN: Right. And this entire concept is supposed to be a five-minute scene?

NAM: Really, I was hoping a restaurant developer would pick it up.

> BIB *chases the other characters except* KEVIN *and* NAM *off.*
> *Music shift.*

KEVIN: Hey, I've been wondering—how come you never wrote anything else about the Farmer after Scene One? If it's the pho show and he's the pho founding father . . .

> *The* FARMER *slowly wanders across the stage, a heavy-looking gánh phở stretching across his shoulders.*

NAM: I mean . . . what's there to say? At some point someone brought pho to Hanoi. That *might* have been him. It caught on as street food for workers. He *might* have been one of those vendors . . . but I dunno. We don't know anything about the actual guy who first made pho, other than he lived in northern Vietnam under colonialism. Let's be real—odds are, he never wrote anything down, stayed poor, and just . . . died.

FARMER: *(sings)* I dreamed—

> *The* FARMER *collapses.*

KEVIN: That's kinda sad.

NAM: Well, we still got his soup. Soup's good.

KEVIN: But we don't have his name. Or his story. You could make something up.

NAM: Yeah, but . . . I should write what I know, right?

> *Beat.*

I can *only* write what I know.

> *The song resumes, once again rubato as when it started.*

(sings) I grappled a long time with drafting this song
I'm unsure that it's apt once again
Was the history captured with interspersed laughter?
Did you learn anything in the end?

Yes, the French once subdued us from ports to the pasture
Entrenching new foods that were forged in disaster
But if I were to name all those munchies with pride
Could you claim the French were . . . justified?

KEVIN: . . . is *that* the takeaway here?

NAM: I don't fuckin' know.

> NAM *sighs.*

(sings) Paris in my sight is shining
As bright as day from far away and never tiring
Oh, my heart will never stray
From those bistros and cafés

Paris, there is no comparin'
Simply the best so all the rest appear as barren
And if it were up to me
French is what I'd wanna be

French is what I'd wanna be
French is what . . . I'd . . . wan . . . na—

(speaks) That's a terrible note to end on—

(sings) In the scraps of the Viet food musical play!

A jazzy piano lick, and a big finish.

SCENE FIVE: MEDIUM PHO

a case study in size insecurity

NAM: Twelve-thirty p.m., March 13th, 2013. Phở Đầu Bò, near Streetsville, Mississauga. My first date. With a *girl*!

Celebratory music cue, or air horn.

It was a low-key date. Eat pho for lunch. Go for a cute winter-time walk. Exist near each other at Tim Hortons. The epitome of romance for awkward fifteen-year-olds. Though of course I was very cool.

AMY: Hi.

NAM: *(to AMY, blurted)* I'm VERY cool!—hi.

(to audience) There she was.

AMY: Here I am!

NAM: This was my first girlfriend. Then my first ex. But we stayed friends. Which is *actually* cool.

They move to a table in the restaurant, where the staff have left some menus, an order sheet, and a ballpoint pen.

So about three years after this date, I showed her the first draft of this scene—

AMY: And I told him he got all the details wrong. For example, he wrote that I showed up earlier.

NAM: But she says I showed up first, then she showed up, then she said:

AMY: *(to NAM)* Sorry I'm late! Had to bike!

NAM: And she says I said:

(to AMY) It's okay, I've only been waiting for, like, an hour.

AMY: *(to audience)* He says:

NAM: *(to himself)* Wait, I don't remember saying that. Was I being sarcastic?

(to audience) She says she thought:

AMY: *(to herself)* Oh god, how could I stand him up like this?

(to audience) I thought he thought:

NAM: *(to himself)* How could she stand me up like that?

AMY: But probably, he thought:

NAM: *(caveman voice)* Ooogh. Pretty girl. Eat food—together![33]

(normal voice, to AMY) So, you hungry?

AMY: *(to NAM)* A little.

NAM: Great. I'm gonna have a phở tái nạm,[34] small. How about you?

  Music starts.

(to audience) I didn't know at the time that she was hungrier than she let on. But she had some misgivings about her order.

AMY: *(sings)* I find myself now at a crossroads
That will determine how our date goes
I find myself at an impasse
Now that he's ordered, I must choose fast

I have a pho routine that I've perfected with my family
But I don't know if I can do the same in front of Nam, he
Might judge me if I show the hungry beast that's deep inside of me
But do I sacrifice my appetite just for propriety?

Oh no, I don't know what to do, if I should take a bet
Oh no, he's looking at me and I haven't ordered yet
I'm showing signs of hunger and I know he must be readin' 'em
But why'd he order small? I'm used to eating medium!

---

33 Alternatively, cricket sounds.

34 A pho with rare beef slices (tái) and well-done beef flank (nạm).

Medium pho[35]
I wanted medium pho
But this bastard must be on a diet or something
I can't explain why he eats basically nothing

Medium pho
God, I want medium pho
But this circumstance calls for an order of small
Even if I think it's nothing at all

NAM: So I always wanted *a* first date for the pho show, but I thought *my* first date wasn't interesting enough to write about until she told her version, and here we are. Thanks to her, I scrapped this pho slow jam I'd been working on, like, "I normally wouldn't do this on the first date, but baby, let's get some hot steamy *fuhh*. *Fuhh* all night long. You should taste this noodle. Spicy. Wet. Meat. Raw. Slurp.[36] What's good for you is good pho mi." That sort of thing. Note the multiple meanings of "good pho mi."

Other patrons and staff in Phở Đầu Bò become a judgmental chorus.

AMY: *(sings)* You never eat
more than your date

> CHORUS: *(sings)* Never eat more
> than your date!

---

35   In the original U of T production directed by Abby Palmer, this chorus was accompanied by two women in the restaurant (Alice Guo and Sara Campitelli) dancing ballet while holding pho bowls.

36   In this role, Kenzie Tsang was partial to ending this bit with an actual slurping sound rather than the word.

That's just the way you play
the game

                              Just the way you play the game

When you're a girl in a world

                              Aaah aaah

In which you can't look fat

                              Fat, fat, fat, fat! You are so fat!

AMY: *(sings)* Do I wait to see the weight he puts on weighing me?
Will my medium give him insecurity
About his *size*—[37]
Would I risk this date for that?

Or do I do the pho routine that I've perfected with my family?
And show the person that I am while eating pho with Nam
He might respect my choices, he's a special kind of boy
He's affectionate and charming, and so cute . . . !

    The music stops.

I can't believe you wrote this, you goddamn narcissist.

NAM: This all happened!

AMY: No it didn't.

NAM: *(to audience)* It's based on true events. Loosely. Can't prove
that she *wasn't* thinking that.

AMY: Are you kidding me?

---

37 A singular dick joke—nothing beside remains, 'round the decay of that
scrapped pho slow jam.

NAM: And if she was, who can blame her?

The music continues.

AMY: *(sings)* Or he could be vain
And I should refrain
Eating more than a man's not endearing
So I've made up a plan, it's adhering

To conventional wisdom
(From a patriarchal system!)
As decreed by the women preceding
That we need to be pleased with conceding . . .

AMY inhales deeply, then launches into a patter.

So we pluck and we paint and we shave off our corners
We nod and we smile and shrink our pho orders
We stretch and we squeeze and slim down, even though
We'll be starving and sad biking home in the snow
And we don't get annoyed, while it's par for the course
That the bar for the boys isn't far from the floor
So why am I the one who has to put on a show
Because this motherfucker doesn't eat a medium pho?!

A pause, then the music softens.

NAM: *(sings)* Hey, are you okay?

AMY: Uh. Yeah.

(sings) And still, no order at all.

NAM passes AMY the order sheet and pen.

NAM: *(sings)* Do you need a menu?

    AMY: *(sings)* No, thank you—

(speaks) It's fine.

    AMY writes down her order, with resolve.

(sings) I'll have a pho dac biet[38] . . . Small.

    A waiter comes to take the order sheet.

. . . Yes, I'll take a small . . .

    A pause. AMY silently watches her order disappear into the kitchen . . . Then the big damn key change.[39]

But I wanted medium pho!

    NAM & CHORUS: You wanted medium pho!

And I ordered a small!

    NAM & CHORUS: And you ordered small!

There's nothing to say now, my choices are lasting

---

38   Literally "special pho." This order has every cut of beef. Amy's pronunciation can be a bit awkward and anglicized; she isn't Viet IRL.

39   Per IRL Kevin's suggestion, singing it up a major sixth in halftime—guaranteed musical knockout.

I have to hold fast to the fact that I'm fasting

NAM: *(sings)* Medium pho!

> AMY & CHORUS: I wanted medium pho!

NAM: You wanted medium pho

> AMY & CHORUS: I wanted . . .

The food arrives. AMY *looks regretfully at an absurdly tiny bowl.*

NAM: *(sings)* But you threw away all of the joys that you knew
For some boy who might never have done it for you

AMY & NAM: *(sings)* I/you wanted medium . . . pho.

Music ends.

SCENE SIX:
PEACE NOODLES

spoilers: communism wins, kinda

Dark music. BACH enters.[40]

BACH: Midnight, January 31st, 1968. Phở Bình, a tiny seven-table restaurant in Saigon, the capital of South Vietnam. I work here. In the daytime I feed American soldiers. Their embassy is nearby. They eat here often. I take their orders. It's a living. And at night I feed *other* soldiers.

My father-in-law came here from the north and set up shop ten years ago, when the French were evicted and Ho Chi Minh took power in Hanoi.

**In case you didn't know: Hồ Chí Minh
Vietnamese Communist leader who fought France and the US; first president of the Democratic Republic of Vietnam (North Vietnam)**

Millions fled from the communists—mostly Catholics and busi-. ness owners, people with something to lose. Phở wasn't big here until they brought their recipes south. Phở's changed here: bean

---

40   Bach's been played in different ways in different productions—as a man or as a woman, solemnly or with a dark sense of humour about it all.

sprouts, basil, lime, hoisin; my father-in-law says you'd never see these in a Northern restaurant. Phở is meant to be delicate, pure; garnishes are decadent. But the Southerners like their decadence. You'd expect that, from capitalists.[41] So we leave a plate of herbs on every table. Of course, Americans have no idea what to do with a bean sprout, so they don't touch them. And the soldiers I feed at night, the ones we hide upstairs, they don't touch them either. Time spent tearing basil is time you could be loading weapons or planning targets, freeing the nation. I do my part by ladling out their soup and keeping them from the eyes of the Southern government. They'll do their part in one hour when they fire the first shots of the Tet Offensive. . . . Happy new year.

In case you didn't know: Tet Offensive
a series of surprise Viet Cong attacks across South Vietnam on
the Lunar New Year of 1968

From where I am, in 1968, I don't know yet that we lose this battle, but I am prepared for it. For death. I am prepared to die when, in three days, they discover the Viet Cong unit based above our restaurant. I am prepared to die when they arrest us, line us up, and execute two of my co-workers on the spot. I will wish that I'd died with my co-workers when the South Vietnamese army spares me just to torture me in a dark cage for years.

Music shift: major key.

---

41 The divergence of Northern and Southern pho kinda parallels the development of North and South Vietnamese arts during the Cold War. The North officially endorsed socialist realism—images and music plainly depicting working-class realities to inspire communist fervour—while the South saw more experimentation with popular and avant-garde styles. As we'll soon see, it's Southern pho that first dispersed into the wider world with the South Vietnamese refugees, while Northern pho is a bit more niche internationally.

But I won't die. I'll live, long enough for our failed offensive to shake America's faith in its war. I'll live, to see Nixon and Kissinger negotiate their exit. I'll live, and I'll see daylight again when we win and topple the Saigon regime, renaming it Ho Chi Minh City.[42] I'll live and return to my restaurant. I'll live through our darkest and most impoverished years, through the reconstruction and US embargo. I'll live to see Ho Chi Minh's successors devise their great scheme to fix our country: capitalism run by the communists, which works, somehow. And I'll live long enough for my sworn enemies, the Americans, to return to our country as tourists.[43] They hear my phở shop has secrets, and they'll pay to learn them along with their overpriced soup. Imagine that—the waiter turned curator, at the restaurant where we sell history. Phở Bình. It's a funny name. You can translate it as "peace noodles."[44]

BACH *waits, then exits. The music ends.*[45]

---

42   This name obviously remains divisive.

43   See also the famous photo from 2016 of Obama and Anthony Bourdain enjoying bún chả in Hanoi.

44   In the last online English-language record I could find of him, a 2010 *Time* article about Phở Bình, Nguyen Kim Bach was still alive and running the restaurant at age seventy.

45   The major-key section of this underscore revolves around a three-note phrase that coincidentally is the same as a popular Vietnamese song written in 1954 called "Xuân Đã Về," or "Spring Has Returned." Wilf wasn't aware of that while writing this music in 2016—mi-so-do also isn't a hard melody to find elsewhere (e.g., in "O Canada")—but maybe Bach would appreciate the happy accident that his main theme is a celebration of the season of rebirth after Tết. Or maybe not, since its songwriter, Minh Kỳ, was also a South Vietnamese police officer that Bach's fellow Communists threw into a re-education camp at war's end. It's complicated!

SCENE SEVEN: LIFE WAS HARD, OR, MY FATHER EATS HISTORY, JUST NOT AT PHỞ HƯNG

three life lessons all wrapped in one hilarious refugee crisis

NAM'S DAD enters abruptly, and says just as abruptly—

NAM'S DAD: Why you have communist in your play?

NAM follows him in, as does NAM'S MOM,[46] probably.

NAM: I think it's a unique perspective—

NAM'S DAD: It's bad!

NAM sighs.

---

46 Having someone play Nam's Mom helps a lot.

NAM: Around midnight, September 18th, 2016. My parents have just driven back from visiting my grandpa in Ottawa[47] and invited me to a late dinner at King's Noodle Restaurant in Toronto's Chinatown, where I moved just two weeks ago.

NAM'S DAD: *(to NAM'S MOM)* Too much bubble tea here now. The Chinese take over Chinatown.

NAM: My mom excuses herself to use the washroom, leaving me to make small talk with my dad. He's not a native English speaker, while years in Canadian public school have left my tongue thoroughly colonized. As such, dinner conversation between us is stilted.

> *Pause. NAM and NAM'S DAD might check their phones a few times, or clear their throats a few times, or both.*

NAM'S DAD: How much you pay for water?

NAM: Everything's included in the rent.

NAM'S DAD: How much rent?

NAM: It's Chinatown.

> *Beat.*

I mean it's cheap—

NAM'S DAD: I know.

NAM: Okay.

---

47   See the book dedication.

Silence.

NAM'S DAD: You have phở since you move here?

NAM: Yeah.

NAM'S DAD: You try Phở Hưng?

NAM: Yeah, I've gone a few times.

NAM'S DAD: What did you think of it? Is it *good*?

NAM: I thought it was okay. Yeah. I liked it.

NAM'S DAD: I never eat there. You know why?

NAM: Yes, I know, it was your first job—

NAM'S DAD: It was my *first job* when I came to Canada!

An up-tempo march begins.

NAM *sighs.*

NAM: My father begins a long-winded story about the hardships of his youth. Of course, I've already heard this story—the last time we ate dinner together.

NAM and his DAD are flung into Saigon circa 1980, with menacing officers around them.

NAM'S DAD: *(sings)* When I was your age, a very long time ago
I got in a mess with the Socialist Republic of Vietnam
I committed a crime, a heinous crime, you know
Called "saying the government's bad in public in Vietnam"

To protest there wasn't allowed
While in Canada, it is a right
So they threw me jail; still I'm proud
That we did and we do give a fight![48]

Life was hard
Life was hard
So I left for Malaysia to get my rights and not lose them
Life was hard
Life was very, very hard
Now you have these rights and you what?

NAM: *(sings)* I do not use them!

(speaks) So, while we've mentioned Tết a few times in the show
already, the real most important holiday in my family is—

NAM'S DAD: December 10th—International Human Rights Day!
Everyone take bus to Washington Vietnamese embassy, protest so
that communist government release political prisoners. This year
is hunger strike!

NAM: Didn't you do enough hunger—in prison?

---

48 Occasionally my mom will cook this vegetable called rau cần, which is
quite good stir-fried with beef, and my dad once expressed his resentment at its
cost in Canada when it was so abundant in Vietnam that he was eating it off the
jungle floor to survive prison. Rau cần is water celery in English, but I wouldn't
be surprised if more people recognized it by the name minari now.

NAM'S DAD: Now it's *my* choice. Maybe you come. If you don't have rehearsal?

NAM: Well, it *is* three months away, so I don't have any plans yet— but I bet I can find some pretty fast.

NAM'S DAD: Your sisters will be there!

NAM: Yeah—'cause they do old people protests and I do fun stuff.

Jump to a boat on the open ocean.[49] *A shark and a pirate enter and battle NAM'S DAD.*

**In case you didn't know: Indochina refugee crisis
the post-war migration of approximately three million
Southeast Asians from the newly communist Vietnam,
Cambodia, and Laos from 1975 to 1995**

NAM'S DAD: *(sings)* When I was your age, I journeyed on a boat
We embarked in the dark, hoping not to see sharks or pirates
All we could do was hope that the boat we were on would float
To the freedom waiting for us if we only desired it

I felt myself dying of thirst
And thousands did not persevere
But I didn't die when my life was the worst
Now I laugh at those days 'cause I'm here—

(speaks) Hahaha!

---

49   Can't you hear the music? That's a 4/4 string ostinato in D minor! Every sailor knows that means death!

NAM'S DAD, the shark, and the pirate march or dance together.

Life was hard
Life was hard
Just look at the trials I faced getting out of Vietnam
Life was hard
Life was very, very hard
I did it so that my three children could feel like their hardships are calculus exams

In case you didn't know:
anywhere from two hundred thousand to four hundred thousand "Indochinese boat people" died at sea

The shark and pirate join NAM'S DAD at his table. They're all friends now.

NAM: *(to audience)* Oh, a dancing shark and pirate duo in a scene about one of history's largest refugee crises. Tasteful! Taste. Pho. Ha. See, I *know* what my dad went through was awful, but it's hard to internalize that. I was taught that history from the day I was born, but even then, it's *history*—I learned it from a distance, probably like you, in my safe little Canadian bubble. Where it's easy to pretend all the world's problems are far away, instead of here and now, sitting across the dinner table.

NAM'S DAD: *(to shark)* You gained weight.

NAM: It's not like you'd *know* my dad's a refugee looking at him. He's a normal person too. He goes to work, comes home, eats rice, then falls asleep in front of the TV. But I remember how for years he insisted that I should stay in swimming lessons, and he would keep asking how long I could swim without getting tired, no matter how many times I answered, over and over.

Pause.

What a kooky guy.[50]

The shark and pirate exit.

NAM'S DAD: *(sings)* Hard, hard, hard, hard, hard
Very, very, very, very hard!

NAM: Bố, you've told me two different stories I already know that have nothing to do with why you don't eat at Pho Hung. Which I also already know.

NAM'S DAD: Oh. Yes. Back to the other story you already know!

(sings) Life was hard
Life was hard
But I didn't come cross the ocean not to get paid
Life was hard

   NAM'S DAD points at NAM expectantly.

NAM: *(sings)* Life was very, very hard?

NAM'S DAD: Good!

---

50   I didn't connect that this wasn't normal dad behaviour until reading *Ru*, the Governor General's Literary Award–winning novel by Kim Thúy, another Vietnamese Canadian refugee. That grade twelve lit circle was a real revelation.

(sings) I landed here in Canada in 1988

 The OWNER *and* WAITERS *of Phở Hưng appear.*

I washed dishes at Phở Hưng until I saw the disrespect
After a week, they underpaid me when they gave me my first cheque
I told the owner, "Where are my tips?" he said—

OWNER: "The dishwasher doesn't get tips!"

NAM'S DAD: *(sings)* And the waiters said—

WAITERS: "You don't get tips? We don't get tips!"

NAM'S DAD & WAITERS: "Then where are the tips?"

(sings) "We want the tips! Give us our tips!"

OWNER: *(sings)* "Listen to me, nobody gets tips!
I am the owner and I keep the tips, and that's it!"

NAM'S DAD: *(sings)* I threw my gloves at that son of a bitch
And yelled, "I quit!"

 NAM'S DAD *and his co-workers make a triumphant marching*
 exit from the restaurant.

And as I stormed out the door, that's when
I swore that I'd never eat Phở Hưng again!
And through all of my struggle and all of my strife
Now, son, you understand how . . .

Big dramatic rubato ending![51]

NAM'S DAD & CHORUS: *(sings)* Hard was life . . . !
Hard life was . . . !

Life!
Was!
Haaaaaard!

Musical button. NAM'S DAD and the CHORUS exit.

SCENE EIGHT: WAITING FOR BÒ KHO

a sad, sad situation getting more and more absurd

Puerto Princesa, the Philippines. A cramped, unkempt barracks or hut for refugees. NHUNG *periodically strums a guitar, bolero-style.* KHANG *minds a simmering pot of phở bò kho on a portable gas stove, sometimes praying silently.*[52] *They do this in the many silences that punctuate the scene, then rapidly quip back and forth.*

NHUNG: . . . Nine hundred and ninety-eight, nine hundred and ninety-nine, one thousand.

KHANG: Good job. Now count back down.

NHUNG: No, that's too much excitement for one day.

Silence.

KHANG: Are you liking the Philippines?

NHUNG: I haven't seen most of it.

---

52   Nhung and Khang are an easy double casting with Nam and Kevin—thus their names.

KHANG: Do you like it here in Palawan, at least?

NHUNG: Do you?

KHANG: It's like a beach resort if you ignore that we're in a refugee camp.

NHUNG: But we are in a refugee camp.[53]

KHANG: I know.

Silence.

NHUNG: I'm hungry.

KHANG: I'm working on it.

NHUNG: Work on it faster.

KHANG: This takes time. Be patient.

NHUNG: Ugh.

Silence.

Did you hear about the lady and the coconut—

KHANG: Oh yeah, she'd just been accepted for resettlement—

NHUNG: In Denmark? So happy—

---

53   I have old family friends who passed through the Palawan First Asylum Centre, though ultimately the choice of setting came down to where the local cuisine was most impacted by Vietnamese refugees.

KHANG: So happy. Then a coconut fell from a tree—

NHUNG: Donk! Dead instantly.

KHANG: So sad.

NHUNG: So sad.

    Beat.

Kinda funny.

KHANG: That's awful.

NHUNG: That's why it's funny.

KHANG: How'd your last resettlement application go?

NHUNG: So sad.

    Silence.

KHANG: What would you think about the UK?

NHUNG: I'd get bored of fish and chips. Australia?

KHANG: I'm terrified of koala bears.

    Silence.

What'd you do today?

NHUNG: Same as yesterday.

KHANG: And the day before.

NHUNG: You know me so well. What day is it?

KHANG: I don't know.

NHUNG: What year is it?

KHANG: When did we leave?

NHUNG: Eighty-something?

KHANG: Let's say it's '88, for good luck.

NHUNG: Would make a good restaurant name.

    Silence.

Do the immigration officers get air conditioning? Or the UN people?

KHANG: I don't think so.

NHUNG: Okay. As long as they're miserable too.

    Silence.[54]

54　I originally had a bit in here revolving around Nhung and Khang singing Elton John's "Sorry Seems to be the Hardest Word," except they get stuck looping that one line about the situation being sad—so sad!—and getting more absurd when they realize they don't know the rest of the lyrics. I don't intend to ruin my enjoyment of Sir Elton's music on the off chance it gets me sued, so I left it out. The *La La Land* guys can come at me, though.

You're Catholic, right?

KHANG: Yes.

NHUNG: How do you pray?

KHANG: Are you gonna start praying?

NHUNG: It'll pass the time.

KHANG: You sit and you think—

NHUNG: I do that already.

KHANG: Think about one important thing and don't think about the others.

NHUNG: Then?

KHANG: Ask God about it.

> NHUNG *makes a half-hearted attempt at praying.*

NHUNG: What does He say?

KHANG: You tell me. Sometimes He doesn't say anything.

NHUNG: Wait, He says . . . "Yes! It would be good to eat soon."

KHANG: Be patient.

NHUNG: That was *pointless*!

Silence.

France?

KHANG: I don't get their movies. West Germany?

NHUNG: If something went down with the East, we'd be toast.

Silence.

I'm hungry.

KHANG: We have a baguette that we were gonna eat with the bò kho, but you could eat it now.

NHUNG: I don't like bread.

KHANG: You *what*?

NHUNG: It's true.

Silence.

You know what'd be horrible?

KHANG: What?

NHUNG: If a typhoon knocked down the tree outside and flattened us both in here.

KHANG: That *is* horrible.

NHUNG: Imagine we made it this far just to die like coconut lady—

KHANG: Can't think about that.

NHUNG: But it could happen.

KHANG: It won't.

Silence.

NHUNG: I'm hungry. Make me instant noodles first.

KHANG: We only have one pot and one stove.

NHUNG: Then why are we wasting them on this?!

KHANG: This will taste better.

NHUNG: It's all the same, noodles and salt.

KHANG: This has beef. And carrots and spices!

NHUNG: *Fancy.*

KHANG: Be patient.

Silence.

NHUNG: Oh, I just came up with a song.

KHANG: A happy song or a sad song?

NHUNG: A song about life in the camp.

NHUNG plucks a single guitar string just once.

It's one-note.

KHANG: Ha.

NHUNG: Ha.

Silence.

Should I make up a sadder story for my next visa interview?

KHANG: Lying is a sin.

NHUNG: I lied in my last one.

KHANG: Then why would it work now?

NHUNG: I'm more desperate.

Silence.

KHANG: You know, the Filipinos learned from us how to make this, but they call it chaolong.

**In case you didn't know: cháo lòng
rice porridge with pork offal**

NHUNG: But cháo lòng is congee.

KHANG: I know.

NHUNG: This isn't cháo lòng. It's phở bò kho.

KHANG: I know.

NHUNG: The ingredients aren't the same at all.

KHANG: I know!

NHUNG: Why don't they say the right name?

KHANG: Some refugee must have told them the wrong one.

NHUNG: Well, some refugee better correct them. It's not chaolong.

KHANG: The name will probably stick long after we're gone.[55]

NHUNG: We'll be here forever.

KHANG: No, we won't.

   Silence.

Japan?

NHUNG: Too polite for my blood. New Zealand?

KHANG: That's not a real place.

   Silence.

Did you hear about, uh, those two—

NHUNG: Oh yeah, what's their names—

---

55   And indeed it did. Palaweños still love to visit a chaolongan to eat their chaolong beef stew, and it's of no consequence that cháo lòng meant something entirely different in Vietnam.

KHANG: They got married!

NHUNG: In the camp!

KHANG: Borrowed nice clothes from the church.

NHUNG: Scraped a feast together.

KHANG: Good for them.

NHUNG: Something to do.

   Silence.

KHANG: Where'd you learn guitar?

NHUNG: Here. To pass the time.

KHANG: Can you teach me? Like I taught you how to pray?

NHUNG: I'd do a bad job. Like you did teaching me to pray.

   Silence.

When you were on the boat, and for a week we weren't sure if we'd survive—did you talk to Jesus?

KHANG: What else could I do?

NHUNG: He say anything?

KHANG: I heard Him—or I felt Him promise that we would make it. And then we did.

NHUNG: But—well, I guess we wouldn't know.

KHANG: What?

NHUNG: If He promised that to anyone who didn't make it.

KHANG: No, we wouldn't.

NHUNG: And you're okay with that?

KHANG: I have to be. Did you talk to Buddha?

NHUNG: No, my ancestors.

KHANG: What'd they say?

NHUNG: "How'd it get this bad?"

KHANG: Ha.

Silence.

I have a nightmare sometimes that the camp gets so full, the whole island sinks into the ocean under our weight.

NHUNG: That could never happen. We're all too skinny.

Silence.

Did you hear about the riot?

KHANG: In the Hong Kong camp? Yeah.

NHUNG: They're trying to send their refugees back.

KHANG: They can't do that. We have rights! We're people too!

NHUNG: They wouldn't do that here, would they?

KHANG: We wouldn't let them. Like in Hong Kong.[56]

   Silence.

NHUNG: I'm hungry.

KHANG: Be patient. It's a special occasion.

NHUNG: Really?

KHANG: Another day we're both alive.

NHUNG: Oh.

KHANG: Also it's my birthday.

NHUNG: Is it?

KHANG: Soon, probably.

NHUNG: Must be about that time.

---

56   See also uc Irvine's online archive of art made by Viet refugees in Hong Kong. Going through it, I was struck by how central the imagery of barbed wire is to many paintings—separating the human subjects from the outside world, in some cases visually cutting through the subjects themselves. Many of Hong Kong's camps were converted prisons and run by the Correctional Services Department, and, unsurprisingly, they treated refugees like criminals.

KHANG: It's your birthday too.

> *NHUNG strikes a major chord to sing "Happy Birthday," and they harmonize—*

NHUNG: *(sings)* Happy—

> KHANG: *(sings)* Happy—

> *They both give up as quickly as they started. Silence.*

KHANG: America?

NHUNG: I'm angry at them. Canada?

KHANG: Are you kidding me? So cold.

> *Silence.*

NHUNG: Did you hear about the ex-captain that just arrived?

KHANG: Oh . . . God. What was it, engine failure on the boat he was taking?

NHUNG: Dozens of people stranded for over a month, no food or water—

KHANG: Why did he have to kill them?

NHUNG: Is it fair to judge?

KHANG: He murdered three innocent people.

NHUNG: I know, one was a kid, but—

KHANG: How can we not judge?

NHUNG: . . . They needed all the food they could get.

KHANG: . . . A Catholic would have offered himself.

NHUNG: He *was* Catholic.

KHANG: A *real* Catholic.

> *Silence.* NHUNG *adjusts his capo and plays the unmistake-able opening chords to "Wonderwall."*[57]

No.

> NHUNG *immediately stops. Silence.*

I miss my mom.

NHUNG: I miss your mom too.

> *Beat.*

Sorry.

> KHANG *glares. Silence.*

---

57 As Tony Aidan Vo sang in a presentation of this scene by the Sống Collective, "I don't belieeeeeve that aaaaanybody's getting out of this refugee camp now!"

Did everyone forget about us already?[58]

KHANG: I don't know. God hasn't.

NHUNG: Do you really believe that? In that salvation stuff?

KHANG: Of course.

NHUNG: That sounds nice. Really.

   Silence.

I'm hungry.

KHANG: I know.

NHUNG: I'm HUNGRY!

KHANG: I KNOW!

NHUNG: Is it done yet?

KHANG: Soon.

NHUNG: But—

KHANG: Be *patient*.

NHUNG: Aaaaagh!

---

58   The crisis had mostly ended in the 1990s, but some Viet refugees were only resettled in Canada in the 2010s.

NHUNG's cry earns no satisfactory response from KHANG.
Beat. NHUNG gets over it.

One thousand! Nine hundred and ninety-nine, nine hundred and ninety-eight, nine hundred and ninety-seven . . .

NHUNG continues to count while plucking his guitar. KHANG continues to pray. The pot continues to simmer. Music.

SCENE NINE:
APOLLO 18 / FRIDAY NIGHT / L.L.B.O.,
OR,
SOUPS FOR A NEW WORLD

pop quiz! guess which country resettled the most Vietnamese refugees in the world, per capita

Music: a sparse piano ballad. TUYET *is alone and morose.*

TUYET: *(sings)* My mistake to pass out on the flight
Now I'm awake, alone inside the night
Last one looking at the sky
It's too quiet out the window of my room
Where I live on the moon

Don't wear regret upon your face
Just be grateful you're not lost in space
I know that's what Ma would say
Here is better than adrift or left marooned
So hide the minor wounds
I live on the moon

And somewhere the sun's still shining
On planets out of sight
I can't go back, I have to look for life . . .

I'll pass out again, then sleep till three
They'll prepare late breakfast just for me
I'll pretend I wanna eat
And my full mouth won't let the empty in me show . . .
'Cause I live on the moon and I'm alone
I live on the moon and it's no home.

> *The music shifts gradually, then all at once to a rock song*
> *tinged with Eurodisco.* DUONG *is with many fellow refugees,*
> *living it up at a restaurant with many drinks.*

DUONG: *(sings)* Won't you think about the kids
Wond'ring what the decades did
New world let our spaceships in
Now we're the ESL-iens

Tomorrow you'll have plans to set
But tonight, don't grow up yet
Our people know the place to be
And you won't be lonely next to me

Friday night, you know the spot
Where drinks are cold and soup is hot!

When the workday wipes away your smile
Let's wreck Ossington a while
New wave karaoke tunes
Will pull you back down from the moon

Heinekens and Hennessy
I'll regret I said "drinks on me"
But if it's sober versus poor
I'm shouting "drinks on me" once more

Oh, that rice cooker can sleep tonight
'Cause you and me, we're feeling—hiiiiiigh
So tell your sponsor family
You'll be out late with the Vietnamese

Friday night, you know the spot
Where drinks are cold and soup is hot!
To the pho shop, you just bring
Your pretty self and then we'll sing—

Ah, ah, ah, ah
Now we're here, it's all alright, all alright
Ah, ah, ah, ah
Oh, at least on Friday night

Friday night, we know the spot
The way we were won't be forgot
Just tell me that you'll love me when
Tomorrow I'm a loser once again . . .

> *The music shifts once more: a sudden, slick beat switch into
> chilly lo-fi hip hop.* THANG *is alone at the night's end, but far
> from lonely. He raps with a laid-back cockiness.*

THANG: *(raps)* Yuh—pho shop paint job still new, word
New world, new boss, ain't you heard?
Self-made steward, say a few words
I be spitting that sriracha at you nerds

Uncle Ho with the new school couldn't fool me
Refugee came through out to the blue sea
With the only French lesson that I ever learned
That only what I own's what I really earn

I look around the city, kids wanna dance
Can't cook, it's a pity they ain't even stand a chance
Working all week on assembly lines
Then spending all their pennies on Henny at night

Well, fine, but I made better plans
Decided I'm supplying the soup and beer cans
Meeting a demand for a Viet canteen
And I'm making no money for a rich white man

I'm a Viet man pimping on my own damn business
Left my homeland packing Vietnam-bition
And a long-term vision, I put that on my kids
They gon' have conditions that I never did

So, Canada, bow down to your new commander
When you come chow down, it's my propaganda
Pho noodle taking over that Toronto scene
A whole twenty years ahead o' poutine[59]

---

59   From what I've found, the oldest Toronto pho restaurant is Pho Rua Vang
on Ossington, dating back to the late '70s. My poutine history is shakier, but it
doesn't seem to have caught on in Ontario until at least the '90s.

So tell young Jenny one day when she wondering
How 'n why ông ngoại built it up from nothing
The sign "L.L.B.O." on the front says
That I'm Lang Liêu, bitch—overcoming.[60]

   THANG hums as the music gently comes to an end.

---

60 If you need to cut part of the show for time, the other two-thirds of this
scene can be sacrificed, but not this rap!

SCENE TEN: PHÖ IS THE NEW RAMEN, OR, WHITE PEOPLE AS THEY TRULY ARE[61]

in which white people think Asian noodles are interchangeable, and Asian people think white people are literally Satan

An INFLUENCER and CAMERA OPERATOR arrive outside a hipster restaurant named "soup." and so do NAM and KEVIN.

INFLUENCER: Oh my god, this is the place!

CAMERA OPERATOR: It's perfect!

KEVIN: Oh my god, this is the place.

NAM: The *heart of evil*!

---

61   People who take extra effort to be wrong and put an umlaut on the word pho fascinate me.

The CAMERA OPERATOR *starts recording the* INFLUENCER.

INFLUENCER: *(to camera)* Hey, foodies of the Internet! We're currently standing in front of "soup."[62]—the hippest restaurant in the neighbourhood of Gentrificationville in the city of Philadelphia.

NAM: *(to audience)* Hey, *Pho* audience in [current year]! We're currently at the beginning of a scene I wrote in reaction to something that was a blip on social media for about two days in 2016. Looking back on it, I don't think there's a deep, nuanced message articulated about gentrification or appropriation in here . . . but it's funny, so I'm not getting rid of it.

INFLUENCER: What's the "scoop." on "soup." you might ask? Well, you uncultured shit, "soup." is a "Southeast Asian BYO."

NAM: Which is to say, it's owned by white people who sell pho for absurd prices to other white people.

KEVIN: *(to audience)* Unfortunately, "soup." got in some hot water—pun intended—after they were highlighted in a foodie magazine's viral video, titled—

INFLUENCER: "Phö is the New Ramen! PSA: You're Eating Phö Wrong."[63]

CAMERA OPERATOR: We'll be all over the socials with this one!

---

62   Please pronounce the punctuation, whether as "dot" or "period."

63   Real video! Look it up! The restaurant and its owner's names are changed here.

INFLUENCER: Teaching kids how to eat "phurrr!"[64]

CAMERA OPERATOR: Kids love "phuwagh!"

INFLUENCER: "Phwong!" The hottest new thing!

CAMERA OPERATOR: "Phwoowy!" The cutting edge!

INFLUENCER: In fact, "phagoogoo" was invented just five days ago!

CAMERA OPERATOR: In San Francisco?

INFLUENCER: San Francisco!

CAMERA OPERATOR: That's where they invented the sushi burrito.

INFLUENCER: Those damn San Franciscans—so creative.[65]

CAMERA OPERATOR: So they must have invented "phwahahahaha"!

The INFLUENCER *and* CAMERA OPERATOR *disappear into the restaurant.*

KEVIN: When Twitter picked up on this, many Viets and other Asians expressed their displeasure with the content.

The ASIAN *ensemble enters, all staring at their phones. Notifications keep dinging in the following section.*

---

64   Ad lib your own pronunciations, as long as they're awful and get worse.

65   The more I think about it, the more I feel like the video production team was probably just too afraid to conduct an interview with someone who had an accent. A San Franciscan accent, of course.

NAM: Why did they choose a white dude as the authority on pho?!

SOME ASIAN: There's no Asian people in the video?

ANOTHER ASIAN: I'm Viet, how's he gonna tell *me* I'm eating pho wrong?

YET ANOTHER ASIAN: Why does pho have to be defined in relation to ramen—

AND YET ANOTHER ASIAN: Too many "trendy" and "exotic" dishes to remember?

GUESS WHO, YUP ANOTHER ASIAN: Why's this guy so anal about putting sauce in your soup?

ANOTHER ONE: all lower case letters and a period. real original branding.

DJ KHALED!: He's clearly just eating spaghetti.

> *The ASIANS disperse and/or become WHITES, wearing blond wigs and contemporary outfits.*

KEVIN: But is it fair that this guy had his restaurant review-bombed on Yelp by dozens of people who've never even eaten there?

> *NAM isn't paying attention, and is instead angrily typing on his phone—*

NAM: "ONE STAR. This restaurant is RACIST and I bet the food tastes like it crawled out a KLANSMAN'S ASSHOLE!"

KEVIN: Nam, he didn't do anything worse than being a white guy who publicly cooks pho and has opinions.

NAM: Go back to opinions about mashed potatoes, bitch!

KEVIN: Just because he's white?

NAM: We're on the same page that this video's *fucking stupid*, right? That title alone—

KEVIN: Sure, but isn't that the magazine's fault? Why are we acting like this *one* dude's takes on this one video are "doing damage" to a community? He's a bit . . . Pretentious, sure, but he's not *evil*.

NAM: . . . Do you *know* that, Kevin?

KEVIN: I guess I don't.

NAM: Well, there's only one way to know fo' sho' fo' the pho show: field research.

KEVIN: *(to audience)* So off we went to "soup."—which went a little something like this—

> NAM *and* KEVIN *enter the restaurant. Everyone inside, all* WHITES, *staff and customers alike, gasps and stares in silence.*

NAM: *(to audience)* We were the only non-white people there. But it's okay, we're used to it. We do theatre.

> NAM *makes a friendly gesture to the* WHITES.

I love . . . craft beer!

The WHITES laugh and ad lib approval, including—

A WHITE: Oh, they're the *good* ones!

NAM and KEVIN sit and look at some very original menus, written on scrolls or something. One of the WHITES takes their orders.

NAM: *(to audience)* I ordered a chicken pho.

KEVIN: And I ordered . . . the broccoli quinoa pho?

NAM: Each of which cost ten dollars American, equivalent to about three thousand forty-seven dollars Canadian.

(to KEVIN) See? E-vil.

KEVIN: That's business. This is an expensive part of town. The owner's gotta make rent somehow.

NAM spots NOAH, the owner/head chef, played by the large white man from Scene Three, in the back of the kitchen.

NAM: . . . Speak of the devil. That's him, right? The chef from the video? God, I can already hear his dumb voice so clearly in my head telling me the "right way to eat pho." His perfect proportions of every garnish. His profound prejudice against the improper use of sauce! How do I get him talking?

KEVIN: Is this necessary, Nam?

> NAM *thinks, then slowly and painstakingly reaches for a sriracha bottle. As soon as he makes contact,* NOAH *whips around and glares. Music.*[66]

NOAH: *(sings)* Wheeeeennnnnnnnnn! people come in and you put the bowl of soup in front of them and they immediately squirt Sriracha and hoisin in, it's like poisoning the chef, oh, don't you see how much it hurts
All my work is all worthless, it turns into dirt, all the thought inside the broth
All the reasoning in the seasoning is lost beneath your sauce!

(speaks) God, do you know nothing?!

NAM: No. Please teach me, senpai!

NOAH: I think I will!

> *The* INFLUENCER *and* CAMERA OPERATOR *start filming* NOAH. *We have entered the world of online foodie content.*

Hey, my name's Noah—Noah Lotaboutpho! And I'm the owner of "soup."[67] the hippest Southeast Asian restaurant in a North American city near you.

> *The music shifts to a chorale, accompanied by organ.*

---

66   The music here is drawn from a traditional melody from the Vietnamese highlands—nah, I'm just playing. For this scene we just stole the incredibly generic guitar chords from the background instrumental of the real "Pho is the New Ramen" video.

67   Brendan Rush, as Noah, pronounced the period as a tongue click, impressively resonant even without a mic.

THE WHITES: *(sings)* Oh, so much in a bowl for such a low price, a marvellous deal
Can I get an amen?
Oh, blessed be the day god granted us this, our holiest meal
Pho is the new ramen

The WHITES get down to a very hokey verse and cooking demo by NOAH.

NOAH: *(raps?)* If we're talking phö, then we better talk ramen too
'Cause we better talk about the things common to
Both dishes, one's a noodle soup from Japan
And the other noodle soup is from a place called . . . uh . . .

Wait, I swear I know this, but forsake it, phö is on the rise
And I'm gonna show you how I take it, I don't compromise
I don't sing this song to say you're eating phö the wrong way
But I'll tell you how to eat the white—the right way!

Ask for extra lime, you can go ahead and slice 'em up
Jalapeño business in the bowl will letcha spice 'em up
My angel, thai basil, go ahead and munch 'em up
Throw in bean sprouts if your noodles don't crunch enough[68]

Now let me reiterate a point I made already
And listening to me would be clever!

A shift to scary organ chords.

---

68   Over several productions of this show, the most important thing we learned is to either buy new fresh herbs for every night or else make some fake ones. The second most important thing is that bean sprouts are always the first to go bad.

Never! Put! Sriracha in your soup!
You'll burn in hell forever . . . !

The music pauses. The WHITES *look mildly concerned.*

(speaks) Hahahahaha! Ha! I'm joking! It's a joke!

Reassured, the WHITES *start laughing along.*

You can do whatever you want with your soup!

On a big, glorious chord—

(sings) You'll burn in hell regardless!

The WHITES *enter a cult-like trance around* NOAH, *who is suddenly possessed by a demon!* NOAH *laughs diabolically as he performs an elaborate ritual, making a blood sacrifice to his dark god from his own body.*[69]

THE WHITES: *(sings)* Oh, so much in a bowl for such a low price, a marvellous deal
Can I get an amen?
Oh, blessed be the day god granted us this, our holiest meal
Pho is the new ramen
Ramen!
RameEeEeEeEeEen!

The music ends, as does the trance. NOAH *drops a bowl of pho on* NAM *and* KEVIN'S *table. The* WHITES *gather around.*

---

69 In the role of Noah, Brendan Rush ripped his shirt open to reveal a penta-gram on his chest, tore a whole lime in half, squirted the juice onto his face, and "cut open" his hand to season his pho with blood. He did great. Now outdo him.

NOAH: Bone apple teeth.

NAM peers into the bowl. A pause.

NAM: This is spaghetti.

NOAH: *(nervous mumbling)* What? No, it's not—RUN! RUUUUN!

NOAH flees while screeching, the WHITES in tow. NAM and KEVIN look at each other.

SCENE ELEVEN:
PIMPING VIETNAM,
OR,
THE SAIGON HUSTLE

in which we get to the point, and get that bread

The "Vietnam Pimpin'" flute melody plays in the background as a re-enactment begins with a businessman wearing a crown.

JEN'S MOM: Once upon a time, there was a Vietnamese businessman. Since arriving to Canada as a young man, he made his money selling cheap bánh mì to his fellow Vietnamese, first in one small Chinatown shop, then eventually in Asian supermarkets across the GTA.[70] But now the businessman was old. He knew he needed a successor, but he didn't know if his three sons were ready to inherit the family business. To prove their worthiness, the brothers set out together beyond the safety of Chinatown, against their father's wishes, to the great wilderness of Queen West. It was here, among the bad and the bougie, that these three would stake their claim to their father's Vietnamese sandwich empire.

---

70   This story is based on a banh mi chain called Nguyen Huong.

Jump to NAM *and* VIP *seated at a table.* VIP *reads through a play manuscript.*

VIP: "When the people you know sit across from your pho, that's how you know that you're home. Lights down. End." Hm.

NAM: This is the Very Important Playwright.

VIP: I'm the Very Important Playwright.

NAM: Really an amalgamation of several Important Playwrights, but one in particular.

VIP: I'm Very Important.

NAM: And he's written many Important Plays.

VIP: I don't pick up the phone for less than a Governor General's Award.

NAM: He wanted that line in the script. What a douchebag.

VIP: The most Important Douchebag you know.

NAM: And today he's giving me feedback on my work! So?

VIP: So . . . White Kevin is funny. White Hipster Satan is funny.

NAM: More white people jokes. Got it.

VIP: So it's funny. Good job. Did you get your Point across?

NAM: My . . . Point? Yeah!

VIP: Good. And what was your Point?

NAM: You know . . .

Beat.

White people are bad.

VIP: White people are bad?

NAM: No . . . that was a joke, I don't wanna make it about—it's about . . . food.

VIP: It's about food?

NAM: Yeah! Food is . . . good. Food is a cultural . . . thing. Culture! . . . is Important, eh? And . . . tasty? Which is all to say . . . white people are bad.

VIP: The Point is "culture is tasty"?

NAM: Yes? No. Why do you keep rephrasing what I say as a judgmental question? And why do I *need* a Point?! Look.

NAM looks out to the audience.

Hey, audience! We're coming to the end of the pho show and we've had some fun times, right? Right? Please, let me hear it if you're enjoying yourself.

NAM pauses. The audience reacts how it will.

Thought so.

(to VIP) And that's the Point. I'm funny.

VIP: Wow . . . is that good enough for you?

NAM: Should it not be? I mean, I wrote some silly soup songs for the drama festival and hoped people would like them. And they did. *Yay*!

VIP: For the school drama festival?

NAM: Yes, the school drama festival.

VIP: But what about now that you're not in the school drama festival?

NAM: Yes I am.

VIP: Are *you*?

NAM: . . . Wait a minute.

> *NAM stares out into the audience again, looking closer this time, and he is horrified.*

NAM: You're not . . . Who the fuck are you people?!

(to VIP) This isn't—what is this?! How did we get here?!

> *A spotlight on NAM. He freezes.*

VIP: *(to audience)* [Theatre Company] presents *A Perfect Bowl of Pho*—a Real Play already in progress—

NAM: No, no no, this isn't—

VIP: Isn't it?

NAM: It can't be—I would've noticed—no, see, Real Plays have a Very Important Point. And I—I—

VIP: Had better come up with one?

The VIP exits. NAM stares, frozen. Jump back into the businessman story.

JEN'S MOM: After one year, the old businessman set out to judge what his three sons had built. It was less than a ten-minute walk from his own shop to theirs, yet they were two worlds apart. Walking down Spadina to Queen, he noticed the sidewalks were littered with no vegetables, the signs carried no pictographs, and the clothes were suddenly much more expensive. This strange opulence was the world his foolish sons wanted to conquer? He chuckled. It was a pipe dream for a simple family like his. Yet he remembered his own youth. He, too, was brave once, leaving by boat to a land far more foreign to him than Queen West was to his sons. *They* had grown up speaking English. The businessman had an accent, even now. And so it was with trepidation that the businessman stepped into the first location of Banh Mi Boys.

Jump back to NAM addressing a town hall of the entire cast of the show, playing various characters from the previous ten scenes.

NAM: So I'm having a problem—apparently the pho show is a Real Play now and this Very Important Playwright says I gotta know what "the Point" is. And . . . I don't know what to tell him. But I figured, no one knows *Pho* better than you guys!

The characters stare at NAM, *confused.*

I know you've all helped me out a lot already, but—

NAM'S DAD *puts his hand up.*

Bố! Yes?

NAM'S DAD: Do they pay you if you get the answer right?

NAM: Uh, not much.

NAM'S DAD: Chết rồi.

NAM: It's just Important now that we find some . . . unity . . . ? Across the pho noodle of time and space. Surely we all have *something* in common?

The characters look around uncomfortably, some mumbling at each other.

LANG LIÊU:[71] . . . Do any of you future people have tips for increasing rice yields?

BACH: Collectivized labour.

NAM'S DAD: Buy it at the supermarket.

---

71 If not limited by double casting, the Farmer can say this line.

BACH and NAM'S DAD glare at each other.

NAM: That's a good starting point! We all have this wonderful Vietnamese cuisine in common. Everybody loves pho—now if we just think about that . . .

The characters mumble in agreement. LANG LIÊU stands.

LANG LIÊU: Actually—hi everyone, I'm immortal king Lang Liêu, young Viet people summon me for help with their extracurricular activities—you've mentioned this "pho" thing a lot, and uh, I didn't wanna be the odd one out, but I actually don't know what that is.

BACH: It's pronounced "phở."

LANG LIÊU: Then why does he keep saying—

NAM: It's not a big deal!—you know, it was well after your time, Your Majesty.

LANG LIÊU: Then why am I here? How am I supposed to help?

NAM: You're the progenitor of Vietnamese cuisine, of course you're here.

KEVIN: But *I'm* not Vietnamese and it's not my cuisine. I just know you.

AMY: Same.

NAM: You guys are Asian.

NOAH: And so am I!

NAM: No!—but, but, you know what? You're all part of a global story of Viet cuisine—oh, I'm onto something—foods moving from one time and place to another—

KEVIN: Creatively adapting to new situations?

NAM: Yeah!

AMY: Diaspora, dual identity, other English major words—

NAM: We're on a roll!

KEVIN: The refugee thing seems Important to you.

NAM: It is! But—what about it?

LANG LIÊU: Resourcefulness, perseverance—

KEVIN: Uh, like your dad!

NAM'S DAD: Hey! It's *my* story!

NAM: Sure! Yes!

NAM'S DAD: *(a revelation)* Ohhhhhhhh! I see it! *The Point!*

NAM: Go for it!

    NAM'S DAD takes the floor to speak. Music.

NAM'S DAD: We started out so poor—the Westerners, the war, we become the refugees—never had anything, they always take it from us. But never, they can never take—

He points at his head

—what's in here. We bring that everywhere, Saigon to Toronto. The spirit. We work hard, harder than anybody, and we create new things to survive. To succeed! Like the first time we ever make the phở—or even the play, okay? We show everyone what is inside us. So when you taste our food, it is a reflection . . . of our human- ity. In the phở is the Vietnamese story. . . of the journey . . . to *freedom*!

The music reaches a triumphant peak.

NAM: Boom! There it is!

The other characters applaud encouragingly for a few moments—with one exception.

BACH: *(with contempt)* . . . Are you kidding me? You're serious?

Everyone turns to BACH, surprised.

Do people actually believe this sort of thing?

NAM: *(to audience, hopeful)* I dunno, do you?

BACH: . . . Oh. I get it. No, you know what? *I* got your Point for you.

NAM: By all means! I'll take notes.

NAM'S DAD: Wait!

BACH: This is the story of you fake Vietnamese who learned to sell out the rest of us.

NAM: Huh?

The music turns more menacing.

BACH: That's what it is, isn't it? You take the one recognizable icon of difference between Vietnam and all the Westerners you play to, turn it into your silly little soup songs, then make a spectacle—of what? The "progress" from us pieces of shit stuck making the soup to the middle-class Canadians who get to write plays in university?

NAM: Oh, word.

BACH: As if there's a common lineage here, so you get to "represent" me and *my* culture—to the halls of power I *fought against*?! No. Maybe the decadent liberals out there can't tell what's off—but I can. I can smell it on you, you—*plate of garnishes.*

NAM'S DAD jumps in, on the verge of physical violence.

NAM'S DAD: Can NEVER trust these fucking Việt Cộng! Don't listen to the communist, it is not "*their* culture" to own—

BACH: What, it's yours? Rich coming from someone who abandoned our country when life got a little hard!

NAM'S DAD: Because you *ruined* the country! I left, start over everything again, and made a good life so my son can write his stupid music play!

NAM: Yeah! Wait.

BACH: Your son exploits our homeland like an American!

NOAH: Yeah! That's me.

KEVIN tries to break it up—

KEVIN: Hey, hey!

BACH: These fucking banana kids always writing about Asia like they know anything—

KEVIN: Just because Nam's a banana doesn't mean he doesn't know what he's talking about—

NAM'S DAD: Don't get into this! You're Chinese!

KEVIN: I'm from *Hong Kong*!

KEVIN ends up embroiled in the fight too, as do others.

NAM: *(to LANG LIÊU)* Oh, Buddha. Your Majesty, could you exert some royal authority over this situation?

LANG LIÊU: Why are you asking me? I don't know much about this modern world, but I do find that "exploiting the homeland" thing a bit #problematic.

NAM: Who taught you that?!

AMY: Exotic food as diaspora metaphor is kinda cliché . . .

NAM: You too?!

The entire room breaks into factions. Ad lib fighting from everyone at everyone else.[72] As this drags on for a while, NAM *loudly talks to himself.*

(dryly) Yaaay . . . I fucking love the Asian identity play . . . !

NOAH, *who's been quiet, suddenly shouts over everyone—*

NOAH: HEEEEEEEEEEEY!

Everyone stops.

I have *no* opinions about this!

EVERYONE ELSE: SHUT UP!

NOAH: Okay!

Jump back to the businessman story.

JEN'S MOM:[73] The first word that came to the businessman's mind as he entered Banh Mi Boys is "modern." The tables, the drink dispenser, the HDTV menu display: "modern." The menu itself, with no Vietnamese writing, listing kalbi beef tacos and kimchi fries three times more expensive than anything the businessman

---

72   If not limited by double casting, Jen should chime in while her mom tries to restrain her:

JEN: I don't know what's going on, but let me call someone bitch! Bitch! Bitch! Bitch! Bitch! Bitch!

73   On a few nights of the 2019 fu-GEN run, Kenley Ferris-Ku played both Bach and Jen's Mom, which is an absolute monologue marathon of a double casting. Bach/Jen is a different combo which might help prevent you from killing one of your actors.

sold: "modern." The ability to pay for his order by card: "modern." He waved a quick hello to his sons in the kitchen before sitting at a table, then observing the people around him, who made him feel, for the first time, out of place in a Vietnamese restaurant. His sons had once described them as "our hip downtown demographic"—beanies were a uniform here and not just for the staff. At least there's always the food, the businessman thought, inspecting his sandwich. Pickled carrots, cucumber, cilantro, all things he put in his own banh mi. Then he bit into it. The meat: pulled pork marinated in Coke. Nothing like anything he'd ever made. But still, a fine sandwich. As he ate, he admired the mural on the opposite wall of an ornate pagoda and cherry blossoms in the sky.[74] How beautiful, and completely meaningless. It was then, all at once, that the businessman understood why his sons chose to build their empire in the jungle of Queen West. In Chinatown, the businessman had been an Asian selling sandwiches to other Asians. But on Queen West, the Banh Mi Boys were Asians selling *Asia* to *everyone*. And Asia was worth far more than a sandwich.

Abruptly—

NAM: So where the fuck is that going?

NAM is alone, addressing the audience more casually.

Hey, sorry, this . . . is gonna be a weird way to end a musical. Just me, talking to you. Just Nam. As portrayed by the very talented [name of actor], but still, me. I just wanted to . . . this ending feels busy and I should get to a Point. I just wanna drop pretenses—say what I'm thinking about. About the pho show.

---

74   The real mural can be found in Banh Mi Boys's location on Yonge rather than the one on Queen West.

Pho—that was a choice. You know, I'm far from the first person to use it as shorthand for Vietnam. That dates back to colonial-era nationalists, who wrote something like, "This soup is ours. It only could have come from our circumstances. As a people, we have something valuable to share with the world." It's a self-selected symbol, but a practical one that we chose to sell everywhere, first to ourselves, then the refugees took it worldwide, and if you're some rando with money, come on in—*bask in the Viet greatness.* I wanted to borrow that energy, render it on stage. That's why it's pho—yeah, there's other Viet foods, but who cares about those? No one's coming to see *A Perfect Plate of Banh Chung*—we eat that at home for the new year. Pho . . . That's the hot commodity. Everyone knows it, it's got *cultural currency*! People would go see that play, bring their own opinions about it. Like, I bet I lost a bunch of white people in the audience with White Hipster Satan, but the rest of you whites are woke, so you're still just angry at how I pronounce "pho." It's the one Vietnamese word you kinda know, and you've already got your lecture ready like, "No! Say a flat, unaccented 'fuh!' That's less wrong! I'm cultured!" Look at you, having thoughts!

. . . I only started having apprehensions when the play started doing well, which is the best time to have apprehensions about your play. And the whole concept of it. Because then these Important Playwrights were asking me, why? What's your message? Have a good answer and you'll have a future. Then all I could see was . . . the shallowness of it all. Suddenly, I felt like I was only elevating the medium through which so many people exclusively view us already: food, especially the transactional kind from a restaurant. That's a shallow medium. Its only message is *flavour*—that doesn't make you care about people. All that history and culture gets compressed into "food taste good, eat more—pay to eat more!" You can imagine a dozen romantic ways to justify it in your mind, but when you strip away the fetishism, it's not immigrant grit, or refugee trauma, or familial love, or hipster trendiness, or the revolution, or woo-woo Oriental authenticity magic that makes pho taste good and keeps you coming back.

Beat.

It's MSG. That's it.

And it's not that I think anyone should be ashamed if they find success making good food. Get that bread. Send me the banh mi. Food doesn't have to be complicated. But this play . . . what is it? If you're just some rando, what's this doing for you? I genuinely wanna know. What are all these jokes and songs, other than . . . a monument to literal consumption? What's the Point? In the end, I only have the answer for me. It's . . . that I'm funny. So give me your fucking money!

VIP enters.

VIP: . . . So that's it? "Give me your fucking money"?

NAM sighs.

NAM: No . . . that's a terrible note to end on.

(to audience) Hey—everything I just said—if you really don't give a shit about it, that's okay. There's still one more song, just for you.

VIP: Oh. The song that makes people cry?

NAM: You know the one.

VIP: After you've said all those other things, do you think it still makes sense?

NAM: Well . . . someone will enjoy it. And that's what matters.

VIP: . . . Is it really?

NAM: Can you give just one straightforward response?!

A pause.

VIP: Yes.

VIP exits.

NAM: Okay. Well, I guess . . . I'm done. So, thank you. For coming to *A Perfect Bowl of Pho*.

NAM exits.

**In case you didn't know: phô
to show off, in Vietnamese**

SCENE TWELVE: COMING HOME

in which the show ends

A Greyhound. Late December. AN, *a university student, rides the freezing bus, still covered in frost and snow. The radio plays.*

GENERIC COUNTRY SINGER: *(sings)* Song about a truck
Song about a truck
All them city boys, oh, they could never understand
My song about a truck

DJ: And that was Generic Country Singer with "Song About A Truck." Next up, we've got—*another* country song! Golly.

AN: No! Make it stop!

Music—a nostalgic country/folk song begins.

DJ: Here's "Coming Home" by Sam Clark, right here on Moose FM . . . Moose FM . . . Moose FM . . .[75]

---

75   IRL, Sam Clark is a fellow Victoria College alum and member of the Toronto folk band Basset. Co-composer Wilf hit him up to guest-write the music for this song for our first run in 2017, and Wilf and I agree it puts everything we wrote ourselves to shame.

AN: *(sings)* The mountains of snow line the old northern roads
They tower from my head to my toe
The heater is broken, and me, I'm just broke
I look like I crawled out a barrel of coke

    AN dusts some snow off her winter clothes.

I'm headin' back south on a dingy Greyhound
To a bus station back in Toronto
And the street lights don't shine 'cause they know they ain't mine
And I'm still such a long way from home

    The chorus melody plays on violin.

GENERIC COUNTRY SINGER: *(sings)* Song about a truck
Yeah I'm still here, I'm still singin' about my truck
'Cause god I, I wanna fuck my truck[76]
Beep beep, vroom vroom

AN: *(sings)* Adulthood came in like a great winter storm
Still, I chose my own way to be torn down
When I picked out a school where white bread was the rule
And I left all the ways that I'd worn out

My mother was quiet on the four-hour ride
Said nothing till the time we arrived
Still the look in her eyes said "I wish that you'd mind
All the people you're leaving behind"

---

76   This was originally an improvised line by Jacob Peng that took the rest of the cast by surprise on closing night of the 2018 Paprika production, and that truck has been fucked every show since.

I hate country music
That's the first thing I learned in North Bay
And I think that I'll vomit if I ever hear again
"Let's all go eat Swiss Chalet"

(speaks) I'm so tired of that restaurant. And Red Lobster! But
they're the only two "fancy" food places north of Barrie.

(sings) Still there's something about it

(speaks) Uh, country music, not Swiss Chalet.

(sings) Something thought out in those lyrics about
Coming home at the end of the day

I'm coming home to you
I'm coming home to you
And wherever I go, this forever I'll know
I'm coming home to you

    AN's parents, who also happen to be NAM'S parents, enter.

The bus and my parents arrive the same time
To the bus station, Dundas and Bay
And all I can think of is how much that I'm
Done with crustaceans and Swiss Chalet

And my dad says "chao con" and my mom says "chao con"
And I say back, "Hello"
Now, god, please, can we go eat
Some motherfucking pho!

(speaks) And my dad says, "Are you sure you don't want Swiss Chalet?"

The entire cast enters.

(sings) Bitch nooooooooooooooooooooooooooooo!

ENSEMBLE 1 & NAM: *(sings)* Bitch nooooooooooooooooooooooo!

ENSEMBLE 2 & GENERIC COUNTRY SINGER: *(sings)* Song about a truuuuuuuck!

Everybody sings together, standing in a line.

ENSEMBLE: *(sings)* I'm coming home to you[77]
I'm coming home to you
And wherever I go, this forever I'll know
I'm coming . . .

Everyone but AN finds a seat at a table.

AN: *(sings)* I'm coming home to you
I'm coming home to you
And wherever I go, know I always miss pho
And I'm coming home to you

And when the people you know sit across from your pho
That's how you know that you're home.

---

77   I feel like this whole song has a bit of Celtic quality to it, pulling from the common DNA of English and French-Canadian folk music. Of course, right here it's sung by a large group of mostly Asians, all on stage at once, which is the Point.

AN joins her family to eat. Lights dim slowly.[78]

The split second before blackout and applause, everyone slurps loudly. Some people in the audience laugh. Some are busy crying. You do you.

End.

---

78   A familiar three-note flute melody here—"Xuân Đã Về," which might be loosely translated as "spring has come home."

Nam Nguyen is a Toronto-based playwright and lyricist of Vietnamese descent. His publisher forced him to write this bio less than a month after he graduated from the University of Toronto, at a time when his only work of note was this one. Nam was named one of *NOW Magazine*'s Breakthrough Stage Artists of 2019 following the premiere presentation of *A Perfect Bowl of Pho* by fu-GEN Theatre Company. His plays have been performed in theatres all across the TTC streetcar network.

First edition: November 2021
Printed and bound in Canada by Rapido Books, Montreal

Jacket art and design by Glenn Harvey
Author photo © Ming-Bo Lam

PLAYWRIGHTS
CANADA PRESS

202-269 Richmond St. W.
Toronto, ON
M5V 1X1

416.703.0013
info@playwrightscanada.com
www.playwrightscanada.com
@playcanpress